LOVE BRUISES & BULLSH!T

It's the toxicity for me.

compiled by
SHEREE SCHONIAN & YASMIN WALTER

Copyright © Sheree Schonian and Yasmin Walter
First published in Australia in 2021
by KMD Books
Waikiki, WA 6169

All rights reserved. No part of this book may be used or reproduced by any means, graphic, electronic, or mechanical, including photocopying, recording, taping or by any information storage retrieval system without the written permission of the copyright owner except in the case of brief quotations embodied in critical articles and reviews.

Because of the dynamic nature of the Internet, any web addresses or links contained in this book may have changed since publication and may no longer be vaild. The views expressed in this work are solely those of the author and do not necessarily reflect the views of the publisher and the publisher hereby disclaims any responsibility for them.

Edited by Andrea Dobbin
Interior design by Dylan Ingram
Proofread by Chelsea Wilcox

 A catalogue record for this work is available from the National Library of Australia

National Library of Australia Catalogue-in-Publication data:
Love, Bruises & Bullsh!t/Sheree Schonian and Yasmin Walter

ISBN: 978-0-6452558-8-1
(Paperback)

ISBN: 978-0-6452558-9-8
(Ebook)

For all the women who aren't able to tell their story.

This is for you.

TRIGGER WARNING:

This book is intended for adults and contains descriptions of workplace harassment, adultery, sexual assault, miscarriages, pornography, financial burdens, substance abuse, death, depression and suicide to name but a few. Some readers may find distressing. Reader discretion is advised.

CONTENTS.

INTRODUCTION. 01 • KEY STATISTICS. 04
FORMS OF ABUSE. 05 • WARNING SIGNS. 07
HOW TO SUPPORT SOMEONE. 08 • SAFETY PLANNING. 12
HAVE A 'GO BAG'. 13 • WHY DON'T THEY JUST LEAVE? 14

POWERLESS.	17	Yasmin
LOST.	27	Sheree
HEARTBROKEN.	41	Emma
USED.	51	Anonymous
JEALOUS.	61	Anonymous
DOMINATED.	71	Dominique
TRAPPED.	85	Cathy
SHAME.	95	Lala
ALONE.	109	Bronwyn
EMOTIONAL.	121	Shel
UNDERESTIMATED.	131	Nicole
CONFUSED.	151	Danni
STUCK.	165	Tanya
REALISATION.	183	AS
INJURED.	193	Anonymous
UNAPPRECIATED.	201	Chris
RESILIENT.	211	Ronnie Joy
UNHEALED.	223	Anonymous
BROKEN.	233	Tigerlily
SURVIVOR.	245	Jennifer

ZONTA HOUSE. 251 • METTLE WOMEN INC. 255
CONCLUSION 259 • REFLECTION 265 • SUPPORT 269

INTRODUCTION.

LOVE
You meet, exchange kisses and you're madly in love. Well, I'm sure it doesn't happen that fast but you are usually sold a dream and quite happily buy into it. There's laughs, there's flirting and there's seduction. You engage in deep and meaningful chats and if you're lucky, heated and passionate sex.

BRUISES
That *LOVE* fantasy bubble has finally popped. He hits you for the first time and you go into shock, questioning yourself, like *maybe I deserved it?* They say love shouldn't hurt so don't forget your colour corrector make-up to hide the bruises from your family.

BULLSHIT
And the gaslighter has entered the building. Once they have smothered you with affection and comfort, they slowly start owning your thoughts. Self-doubt kicks in because they've made you feel crazy. Then, on top of that, the bullshit promises and the empty words start to regurgitate out of their mouth. 'I am sorry. I won't do it again. I only hit you because I love you so much. I just lost it – I don't know what happened. You made me do this. It was the alcohol. I'm sorry, you know I love you. You provoked me.

I was having a bad day. Please come home, I promise I won't raise my hand again.'

> 'Sometimes it lasts in love, and sometimes it hurts instead.'
> – Adele

ABOUT THE AUTHORS

Sheree Schonian is a survivor of domestic violence who is now dedicated to being an advocate for families navigating through the trenches of family and partner abuse. During her campaigning, Sheree was often met with ladies too afraid to speak up in public, but felt connected enough to share their story in confidence. Believing that together we can make a difference, Sheree teamed up with her sister Yasmin Walter who is an established author and publisher. They then put a call out for brave women to share their stories.

Alongside their own personal stories, Sheree and Yasmin are joined by eighteen other survivors of domestic violence for a real-life memoir. They have drawn upon their experiences, unpacked their trauma and share the conversation with those who have also lived their own pain.

Some stories are shared from the survivors' perspective, some from the child who grew up in a home filled with violence and even those who have lost family members at the hands of their partners.

These stories are powerful, and unlike many families, these ladies were lucky to leave still breathing. They're hoping with these stories, they can highlight the severity of domestic and family violence and how the system is failing those begging for help. These sisters strongly feel these conversations can save more lives and be used as a push towards getting legislation updated.

Domestic violence shouldn't be a taboo topic. We need to strip shame away from it and have those heavy conversations to save more lives. It's so beautiful to see family and domestic violence coverage extend onto mainstream TV like Netflix's *Maid*. A great series that highlights that abuse isn't always physical and there is a lack of support for those wanting to escape and rebuild their lives.

OUR MISSION *for this book is to educate, motivate and advocate in the community to stand up and stop violence against women, men and children. To make a difference and lead the way for a positive change to occur. We hope to raise the vibration for future generations and teach people to identify what a healthy loving relationship is.*

Part proceeds of this book will also directly benefit Mettle Women Inc., a charity dedicated to rebuilding the lives of family and domestic violence survivors

Violence against women is any act of gender-based violence that causes or could cause physical, sexual or psychological harm or suffering to women, including threats of harm or coercion, in public or in private life.
– UN Declaration

KEY STATISTICS.

On average, one woman a week is murdered by her current or former partner.

- 1 in 3 Australian women (30.5%) have experienced physical violence since the age of 15.
- 1 in 5 Australian women (18.4%) have experienced sexual violence since the age of 15.
- 1 in 3 Australian women (34.2%) have experienced physical and/or sexual violence perpetrated by a man since the age of 15.
- 1 in 4 Australian women (23%) have experienced physical or sexual violence by a current or former intimate partner since age 15.
- 1 in 4 Australian women (23%) have experienced emotional abuse by a current or former partner.
- Australian women are nearly 3 times more likely than men to experience violence from an intimate partner.
- Almost 10 women a day are hospitalised for assault injuries perpetrated by a spouse or domestic partner.
- Women are more than twice as likely as men to have experienced fear or anxiety due to violence from a former partner.
- Almost 1 in 10 women (9.4%) have experienced violence by a stranger since the age of 15.

(Source 2021: ourwatch.org.au)

FORMS OF ABUSE.

Abuse in relationships, which is also called domestic violence, is any behaviour that causes physical, sexual or emotional damage, or causes you to live in fear.

Non-physical forms of abuse can be just as damaging as physical violence.

EMOTIONAL ABUSE
When someone:
- constantly puts you down or criticises you
- threatens to stop you from seeing your children
- threatens to commit suicide if you leave the relationship

SOCIAL ABUSE
When someone:
- prevents you from seeing your friends and family
- makes you feel guilty about going to work or socialising
- constantly checks up on your whereabouts

FINANCIAL ABUSE
When someone:
- takes control of your financial affairs when you don't want them to
- prevents you from having access to money

SEXUAL ABUSE

When someone:
- makes you do sexual things that you don't want to do. Forcing you to have sex is a criminal offence, even if you are married

STALKING

When someone:
- follows you around, or repeatedly tries to contact you, even if you've said you don't want this

PHYSICAL ABUSE

When someone:
- pushes, hits, throws objects, drives dangerously to frighten you
- threatens to physically harm you, other people, or pets

(Source 2021: relationshipsnsw.org.au)

WARNING SIGNS.

If you're worried you may be a victim of domestic and family violence, think about your relationship, your feelings and your partner's behaviour. If you answer yes to any of the following questions, it's likely you're a victim.

Keep in mind, this is not an exhaustive list. There are other types of domestic and family violence people can experience.

- Do you feel that you're often 'walking on eggshells'?
- Is it difficult to disagree with or say 'no' to your partner?
- Does your partner check up on what you're doing?
- Does your partner try to stop you seeing friends and family?
- Does your partner accuse you of flirting with other people?
- Does your partner dictate how the household finances are spent, or stop you from having any money for yourself?
- Does your partner pressure you to do things you don't want to?
- Does your partner threaten you, push you, damage property, throw things or make you feel unsafe?
- Do your children hear or see things that might be damaging to them?
- Does your partner threaten to kill themselves, or take the children away from you?
- Have you been frightened for your own or your children's safety?

(Source 2021: relationshipsnsw.org.au)

HOW TO SUPPORT SOMEONE.

It is okay to say something if someone you know is experiencing domestic or family violence.

HOW CAN I SUPPORT SOMEONE?

Finding out that someone you know is being hurt is always hard. Perhaps you want to help but don't know what to do. The good news is that there are simple things you can do that can make a big difference.

When someone you know is experiencing domestic or family violence, the way you talk and listen to them makes all the difference. You may be worried about doing the wrong thing, but it is important to know that it is okay to say something. Many people are glad to have the chance to talk about what they are going through.

When someone is experiencing violence they often feel trapped and out of control. These feelings can be made worse if you try to force them to do what you think is best. It is very important that people are supported to make their own choices, when they are ready.

Here are some ways you can help:
- In an emergency or if someone is in danger, call 000 immediately
- Believe them and take their fears seriously. This is important no matter what you think of the person or people who hurt them
- Listen without interrupting or judging

- Never blame the person experiencing the violence for what has happened to them. Violence is never okay
- Don't make excuses for the person who has hurt them
- Understand that they may not be ready, or it may not be safe to leave. Don't try to force them to do what you think is best
- Remember that domestic and family violence is not just physical
- Help in practical ways, with transport, appointments, child-minding or a place to escape to
- Help explore options. You or the person you are supporting can call 1800RESPECT or visit their website *(1800respect.org.au)* for more information and support
- Some people may need the help of an advocacy service to explore options. You can find an advocacy service in your area by searching the service directory on their website *(1800respect.org.au)*

'When someone you know is experiencing domestic or family violence, the way you talk and listen to them makes all the difference.'

WHAT ARE THE SIGNS OF DOMESTIC AND FAMILY VIOLENCE?

People experiencing domestic or family violence may:
- Suddenly stop going out with no reason
- Worry a lot about making a particular person angry
- Make a lot of excuses for someone's negative behaviour
- Have marks or injuries on their body that can't be explained
- Stop spending time with friends and family
- Seem scared or wary around a particular person
- Seem worried that they are being watched, followed or controlled in some way

A person whose behaviour is violent or abusive may:
- Act in ways that make the other person scared
- Put the other person down all the time
- Make threats to hurt another person
- Control:
    - Where someone goes
    - Who they see and speak to
    - What happens to their money
    - How and when they can use their phone, car or computer
- Have a lot of rules about how the other person is allowed to behave
- Get very angry when the other person doesn't follow these rules

HOW DO I ASK SOMEONE ABOUT DOMESTIC AND FAMILY VIOLENCE?

In the end, the only way to be sure there is a problem is to ask. This might feel hard, but there are things you can do to make it easier.

You may be worried that the person experiencing the violence will get angry, upset or won't want to talk. This may be the case, but often people are glad to be able to talk about what is happening.

Pick a quiet time to talk, when the violence isn't happening. Let the person talk at their own pace, don't push them to say more than they feel ready to.

If the person you are talking to doesn't react in the way you hoped, don't take it personally. Let it go for now, but let them know you are there if they need you.

It's better to talk to them about the things you've noticed that make you worried, than to give your opinion.

You can try some questions like:
- I'm wondering if everything is okay at home?

- I noticed you have some bruises. How did that happen? Did someone do that to you?
- I've noticed you seem frightened by your partner [or other person you suspect is hurting them]. Is that right? Is everything okay?

Give them the chance to speak in private. Be prepared to listen, but don't force them to speak if they are not ready.

(Source 2021: 1800respect.org.au)

SAFETY PLANNING.

You can make a simple safety plan for yourself, with help from a friend or someone in your family. You can also contact a support service for help making a detailed safety plan. Every plan is different as every person has different needs. It's a good idea to create a new safety plan as things change, for example if you move house or leave your relationship.

If you are making a safety plan for yourself, you will already have good ideas about things you can do when you feel unsafe. These might be as simple as contacting a friend when there is violence where you live. You can start your safety plan by writing these ideas down. Keep your plan somewhere that no-one else will see it. You might choose to share your safety plan with a friend or other support person. Let them know you may be calling them if you feel unsafe at home.

Support services can help you think about actions you can take when you feel unsafe. Contacting a support service to make a safety plan is the best place to start if you are living with sexual assault, domestic or family violence.

> 'Staying safe does not mean changing your behaviour so that someone doesn't get angry. You are never responsible for another person's violence.'

(Source 2021: 1800respect.org.au)

HAVE A 'GO BAG'.

A 'go bag' or escape bag should contain essentials you'll need to take with you if you have to leave in a hurry. If you can't keep this bag hidden at home, ask a loved one or neighbour to hold onto it for you.

Your 'go bag' might contain:
- Money
- Spare keys
- Phone charger
- Clothes for you and children (if applicable)
- Essential toiletries (e.g. toothpaste, toothbrush, sanitary items)
- Medications and prescriptions
- Passport and licence (or copies)
- Contact numbers (e.g. friends, family, support services)
- Copies of important documents (e.g. birth certificates)

(Source 2021: raq.org.au)

WHY DON'T THEY JUST LEAVE.

It can be devastating to see a loved one in an unsafe relationship. It can also be difficult for an outsider to understand why a victim of domestic and family violence doesn't leave the relationship.

Abusive relationships can be complicated – especially if kids are involved. It's not always safe for a victim to leave their abuser.

In fact, the most dangerous time for a victim of domestic abuse is right after they've left their abuser. They can put themselves and their children at serious risk.

It can take a lot of time, planning, support and courage for someone to escape an abusive relationship. And even if someone does choose to leave, there's a chance they may return.

On average, it takes someone up to **7 times** to leave an abusive relationship before they get out for good.

It's important to keep this in mind if you're upset with yourself for returning, or if you're becoming frustrated with the 'back and forth' of someone you know who is living with abuse. With continued patience and support, the victim may grow more confident in their decision to leave.

There are many reasons why someone might stay in an abusive relationship, such as:

- They may be embarrassed or ashamed to tell friends/family about the abuse
- They and their children may depend on their partner financially
- They may have a disability and depend on their partner physically
- They may be afraid of coping on their own
- They may blame themselves for the abuse
- They may have damaged self-worth and think they deserve the abuse
- They may have grown up witnessing abuse and thinking it's normal
- They may have emotional ties to the abuser and hope the abuser will change
- They may be worried about where they and their kids will live
- They may not know their legal rights
- They may be worried about child custody arrangements
- They may want their children to grow up with both parents
- They may be receiving pressure from their family or community to stay in the relationship
- They may not know about the available support and resources that can help
- They may be afraid their abuser will become violent toward them, their kids or their pets if they try to leave

These are just *some* of the reasons someone might stay in an abusive relationship. It's important to remember that it's not always safe for someone to leave their abuser.

(Source 2021: raq.org.au)

POWERless

POWERLESS.
Yasmin

The smell of guava makes me quiver. The sweet floral scent has been tarnished with violence. My siblings and I were playing in the front yard when my stepdad hastily pulled up in the driveway and aggressively questioned us on the whereabouts of our mum. He stormed inside, and as a seven-year-old child wanting to protect her mum, I followed him in. That's when the smell of guava hit me and established the connection of smell with sight. A bowl of guavas had been thrown against the wall, spraying the fruits and strong scent across the kitchen. I found my mum. She was in the corridor in the fetal position as my stepfather was booting her in her ribs with closed shoes. 'STOP! STOP!' she yelled but that didn't seem to deter him.

As a survival mechanism, I have compartmentalised a lot of the violence I saw as a child. I can't quite recall how it all started but I do know my mum, my siblings and I lived in fear for a very long time at the hands of my stepfather. I saw things that NO innocent child should ever have to witness. We often went without, as Mum struggled to provide for her five kids. We lived in public housing as all our family were overseas, so we relied on relief from women's refuges. Again, memories are not clear, but I recall thoughts of happiness and safety. We knew that for a week or two, we would be free from harm's way. We knew that we wouldn't be woken up in the middle of the night to Mum's pleads to stop. I remember making a colourful wind chime out of paddle-pop sticks. I was so proud of my creation and the encouragement that came with it. The ladies there were so kind and helpful, and they went out of their way to keep us entertained with art activities, book readings and warm hugs.

On one occasion when we were on the run, the refuge was full that night so they couldn't take us in. We had no choice but to go back home and drive our car into the backyard so he wouldn't know that we were home. We lived in a really old house, full of cockroaches and with an outside toilet. I needed to go to the toilet in the middle of the night but I was too afraid to go outside in case he was there so I peed in the bathtub. Not going to lie, after that experiment I continued to do that until they eventually built an indoor toilet for us. Though I think that's how I became really good at squatting, lol.

Mum was on and off with him for years. She stuck by him through the hospital trips, the VROs, the police visits, the cheating, the lies, the beatings – you name it. Again, I don't have any clear memories of how it ended, but it did. I did ask my mum recently and she told me he had found another woman and moved on. And speaking of moving on, my mum introduced us to her new boyfriend a couple years later. I *HATED* him. He had done nothing wrong, but I just hated him. I was a broken tween girl with no interest in Mum having a new man in her life. What if he was the same? Was he trying to be my new dad? My relationship with my biological dad was also *meh* so the last thing I wanted to deal with was another wannabe father-figure. I was bad. I was *soooo* mean to him. I pushed him away and made everything difficult. He did so much for us, and he was so gentle with Mum. He took us to restaurants, to parks, to the Royal Show, to the movies – you name it. He spoilt us but I still hated him. I can look back and laugh at it because I now know I was acting out in pain. But he never gave up on us kids and kept trying his hardest to win us over, and he eventually did.

Now, I don't know what it is with me and the toilet, but when I was on the toilet, I heard yelling and I just knew straight away it was him. He was back. My sister came running into the toilet and locked the door. My old stepdad and my new stepdad were having a fistfight. My old stepdad took his two biological kids with him that night and they never returned to live with us again. My mum was deflated and absolutely heartbroken. We all were. And she never once yelled for help whenever she was getting beaten up. She didn't want her kids to come anywhere near the violence. She tried her hardest to protect us from violence, but my two youngest siblings were directly affected this time and began their new life with their dad. I have to say, though, despite everything he did to my mum, he never raised a hand at us, and treated us with the same affection as he did his own children. However, as kind as my new stepdad was, it didn't last. My mum had her guard all the way up, anticipating deceit and heartbreak. She continues to feel distrust towards all men, which has really destroyed the foundations of any new relationship she enters.

Statistics suggest that children who grow up in an abusive environment generally gravitate towards similar situations in their

> **WE NEED TO ACKNOWLEDGE THE RED FLAGS AND NORMALISE LEAVING AN UNHEALTHY RELATIONSHIP – ESPECIALLY WHEN KIDS ARE INVOLVED.**

adult relationships. This became a reality for my eldest sister. She hid the abuse very well. She became distant with our family to hide the bruises and to keep us safe from his bullshit. He kept her under control with threats to harm her family – US. We had an inkling that she was in an abusive relationship but she pushed us away any time we asked. To avoid completely losing her, we stopped asking questions. Straddling her strength to survive for her two children, something finally clicked and she left him. I took her into my home, and as a family, we helped her rebuild her life. That brave life decision she made was bigger than saving herself from torture. At that point she taught her almost-teenage daughter that this behaviour is unacceptable. It's unacceptable to be treated that way by a man who says he loves you.She also taught her young son that treating the woman you love with such disrespect is unacceptable.

I am now aware that breaking the cycle is important. Breaking generational habits has to start with someone. I have made that commitment to let it end with me. All my ex-boyfriends were bad boys. I don't know if that was just my teenage hormones that found bad boys so thrilling, but there is just something about feeling protected by a bad-ass that is so sexy. I dated gang bangers, drug dealers and just straight-up losers – *HA!* I was always in control and had these tough boys wrapped around my finger. However, I too could have ended up a victim of domestic violence if I didn't end things with the frog before my Prince Charming. He was starting to get controlling with his ways. He would go through my phone, through my phone bills (calling every number he didn't know), take my ID so I couldn't go clubbing (dumb dumb forgot about my passport so your girl was still hitting the clubs *#sorrynotsorry*). Drug-induced paranoia would kick in and I'm suddenly 'having affairs with every Tom, Dick and Harry'.

If we argued, he would smash things around the house but he never once laid a hand on me, even with my really big mouth and provoking words. During an argument, he decided to break up with me. I took that opportunity to leave and never look back. And that's when I decided that I would never put myself in a situation like that again.

I had to grow up really quickly. With that, I learned how to be confident, defend myself, and most importantly, protect myself. I was a modelling teacher and my class had been invited to participate in a fashion show. I needed more boys so I asked my sister if she had any friends who would be keen. She sent her best friend's brother and *DAMN* he was fine. I came back that day, dramatically fell onto the couch and said to my sister, 'I'm going to marry Mr Yummy.' Two years later I was Mrs Yummy. He bought the ring after six months of dating, at the young age of nineteen. I walked down the aisle to Beyonce's *Halo*. '*Remember those walls I built, Well baby they're crumbling down,*' because that is exactly what happened. He was such a gentleman. So kind and loving. Super hot, *ohh*, and he had a *touch* of bad boy (in a good way, like stand-up-for-himself-and-his-friends-in-the-nightclub kind of vibe, not ohh-look-at-me-I'm-so-tough)! But just like my mum, my views on men had been tarnished. In the beginning of this relationship, I would try to start fights and bicker with him but he wouldn't budge. I was used to arguing, so it felt weird not to. He is three years my junior but far more mature than me. We have been married for ten years now with two beautiful girls. He showed me that relationships can be positive and non-toxic. And I showed him that it's okay to be loved. We both come from broken homes, but we have built a strong foundation for our girls, which we are proud of. Yes, my husband and I were raised on heartache, but we are okay, and we are thriving. We have broken the cycle!

A few months ago, I accepted an award from Ausmumprenuer for the category Women Who Will Change the World. I was honoured to be recognised for the significant difference I have made with my book *The FIFO Wives' Tales*. Winning first place meant that the trophy came with responsibility. And responsibility requires action. Single-handedly I know I can't change the world, but I can be a role model and make a slight difference. And it all starts with kindness. The world needs more love. If I put a smile on someone's face today, not only does it make them feel good, but it will cause a ripple effect of happiness onto the next person and so on. Bad decisions come from stress, pain and anger. And it all starts at home. I teach my children how to be respectful, be kind and always lend a helping hand. The most important virtue I have taught them is how to be loved and how to love. Growing up in a household of family violence, love and happy times is not something I was raised with, so I was adamant about breaking the cycle. I have received many compliments throughout my life, but someone made a comment that constantly plays on my mind. She said, 'Look how happy and well-behaved your children are. You can tell they are loved.' And for me, that's more important than their grades or their sporting achievements. I value how they treat others.

If you're reading this and you are staying in your abusive relationship because you want your kids to have their parents in the same household, trust me when I say this: *they do not want it.* Sure, the idea of it is nice, but they want their mum to be happy and safe. Kids know a lot more than we give them credit for, and they can read situations as well as adults. I may not have a crystal-clear memory of what happened in my childhood, but it has definitely affected my life in more than one way. Do I wish my mum left that situation earlier? Absolutely. I think of my seven-year-old daughter now, and it breaks my heart to think about her witnessing that. The innocence of a child is ripped out of their core, leaving them traumatised. And that's how the cycle continues.

As I got older, I started to understand more about trauma, how humans behave and why they behave that way. Not taking anything away from the victims, but the abusers simply did not know any better in most cases. Most behaviours are learnt or mimicked. If someone is not taught how to be respectful, it's unlikely that they could reciprocate that. If someone is neglected or abused in early childhood, they often create protective walls which prevents them from being able to love others on a conscious level. If someone is not shown that they are loved, they simply cannot love. Throw in substance abuse and it's a whole different ball game. The negative emotions, fears and built-up anger needs to leave the body, and unfortunately, it's often directed at the partner.

It's not fair that we have to teach our daughters to practice safety. Simple activities like walking in the park alone at night sends a shiver down my spine. Women are constantly living in fear. We need to educate our sons. Show them how to respect women and listen to their opinions. Remind them that *NO* means *NO*, and sex must be consensual – even if she is his girlfriend. Teach them that loving someone is a cherished feeling. Demonstrate what a healthy relationship looks like. Help them understand that abuse is a crime. Encourage them to speak up if they see their peers being abusive. Inspire them to be helpful and kind to others. Let them know that, yes, porn exists, however, it is not real and doesn't represent a solid or functional relationship.

POWERLESS.

Here is a letter I wish I wrote my mum when I was a kid.

Mummy.
I'm sorry.
I'm sorry I can't help you.
I'm sorry I'm too small to get him off you.
I know you want to stay with him so we can be a family.
But, Mummy, I don't want this.
And neither do you.
I don't want to see you cry.
I don't want to see you hurt.
It's scary when Daddy yells.
It's scary when things break.
You tell me that everything is okay.
You tell me that you are fine.
I know that you are always scared, and that smile is a lie.
But Mummy I know you are.
And the truth is so am I.
I don't want to wake up one day and be told that you are gone.
I don't want to live a life without my mummy by my side.
It's okay to leave Daddy I promise I won't be mad.
It's okay to keep us safe and protect us from the bad.
You know we see the bruises.
You know that we aren't blind.
I know it's hard to leave, however it's the time.
Because, Mummy, we need you to save us.
I'm sorry.
I'm sorry, but you need to save us.

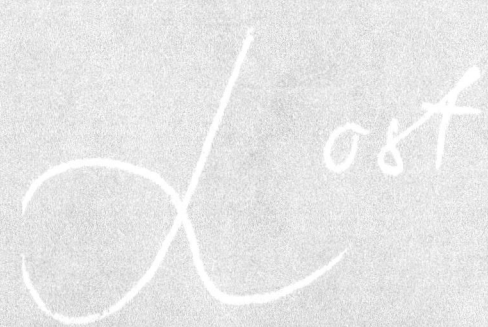

LOST.

Sheree

'**G**et away from her or I will kill you!' I yelled as loud as I could whilst holding a kitchen knife tightly in my hands, ready to stab a grown man for hurting my mummy. Not that I could have done much damage since I was only nine years old, but it was all I could think of doing to protect my mum from being beaten to within an inch of her life, once again. He didn't stop. He looked at me and continued to hit my mummy. So, I ran towards him with the knife still in my hand, which had gone white from gripping it so tightly – I was so close to getting him. I wanted to hurt him, like he did my mummy, only to suddenly feel someone grab me and pull me back. *What the in world?* I was so focused on getting to him, I didn't even realise that our next-door neighbours had somehow gotten into the house to help stop the commotion. As Aunty Sandy grabbed me and forced me to drop the kitchen knife, Uncle Simon had gone to try and stop him from hurting my mummy.

I don't know what really happened after that except there was a lot of commotion and yelling, but what I do know is I was smacked on the bottom and yelled at and sent to my room. It wasn't my mum that smacked me, but him. She was in so much pain and bleeding from her face, that she couldn't move or do much to stop him, she just had to let it happen.

Although this was the only time he smacked me, the beatings of my mummy continued for years and years. As I was the oldest of my mum's children, I had to become my siblings' protector from seeing the abuse and become their mother. I was a young girl who had to grow up so quickly to care for everyone.

> **THE LESS WE TALK ABOUT DOMESTIC VIOLENCE, THE MORE WE HAVE TO LOSE.**

By the time I was ten years old, I knew how to cook, clean, do grocery shopping and make adult decisions for my siblings. I lost my entire childhood. I never got the chance to be a child. Well, actually maybe I did, but because I have suppressed so much of my childhood so I don't remember the violence, I couldn't even tell you. My sisters and I very rarely talk about the past. Each of us seems to have a different memory of what happened. Sometimes they don't remember the things I remember, or I don't remember what they have remembered. I do hope that in some way, shielding them from some of the violence is why they don't remember what I do. Our childhood was not an easy or pleasant one, but it has made us the women we are today.

I was a lost young sixteen-year-old girl who didn't feel loved when I met Nick. Nick was everything I didn't have in my life. He showered me with love, compliments, attention and gifts. I thought I had hit the jackpot. He was the guy every girl dreams of, well, so I thought. The abuse didn't start off being physical. It started with sly comments about what I was wearing, where I was going, who I was with, why I was late. I just brushed it off as him wanting me to be safe because he loved me and didn't want me to get hurt. The first real sign I should have noticed that said something wasn't right was when he tore up my year twelve ball photos in my bedroom. I had gone to my ball with my ex-boyfriend, and I guess he was just jealous, but of course I blamed myself for keeping the photos. I yelled at Nick for ripping them up. He got angry and stormed out of the house. I quickly gathered myself and ran after him. I didn't want him to leave me, although now I wish I just let him go.

Things seemed to be going okay after that, until one day my ex-boyfriend called me to tell me that my phone bill had arrived and I needed to pay. You see, he had signed a contract for me in his name so I could get the phone. When Nick found out that my ex-boyfriend called me, he flew into a jealous rage. He didn't care what the reason for the call was, just that I was talking to my ex.

He began to scream at me. Calling me every name under the sun. I tried to explain repeatedly that the call was simply about a phone bill, but he didn't care. I gave up trying to explain. I had turned my back to walk away when Nick grabbed my arm, spun me around and slapped me hard across the left cheek. I felt a stinging sensation as his open hand made contact with my face. I stood there in shock. I had never been hit across the face before in my entire life. Whilst standing there, it seemed as if something had suddenly switched on in Nick. As in – he liked this. He liked to hit girls. Maybe it made him feel more powerful or whatever, but instead of apologising to me for what he had just done, he went the other way. He lunged at me. Grabbing me by the hair, he pulled my face up to look at him and told me if I ever spoke to my ex or any other man again, I'd be done for. *What the fuck is happening?* I thought. *Where has my loving boyfriend gone?* I tried to get away. I pulled at his hands to let go of my hair so I could get away. I managed eventually to somehow pry his hands apart and made a run for it. I ran to his friend's apartment. Yelling, crying and begging for someone to help me and to stop him, but all I got were looks. Looks like, *We aren't going to do shit because it's not our business. We are going to stay out of it.* I couldn't believe it. Those guys were condoning his behaviour. Allowing this to happen to me, like it was completely normal. What a bunch of [insert your own word here] …

I managed to get into the bedroom where my stuff was only to have Nick follow me there. *Shit!!* I had no idea what was about to happen. He started yelling and swearing at me again and was just being so mean. I just stood there sobbing. Man, my cheek was hurting badly and was beginning to change colour. Going from red to a more blue-black colour.

Luckily, after what felt like an eternity, one of Nick's mates came in and told him that it was enough and to stop. *Thank fuck!!* Finally, someone had the balls to come put a stop to this. I quickly ran past Nick and his friend and bolted for the front door but where was I to go? How was I meant to get home? I had no car, no money. I definitely could not have called my mum to get me. So, I just sat on the curb. Waiting for some Prince Charming to come and rescue me. *Ha!* What kind of fairytale thinking is that? Of course, no Prince Charming came, only Nick. This time, though, he seemed different. Not the Nick that was yelling and screaming and the one who slapped me, but the Nick who loved me. Nick came and sat down next to me and pushed my hair out of my face. I looked at him. My eyes were all red, puffy and sore from crying and I saw that his eyes were starting to swell with tears as well. He ran his hand over my left cheek and began to sob.

He told me he was *sooo* sorry and that it would never happen again. That he was just so angry and thought I was cheating on him and that I was going to leave him. He told me he loved me so much. He also managed to somehow blame me. Saying that if I didn't talk to my ex none of this would have happened. I just nodded and cried some more. Nick said he would take me home so I could get some sleep. It wasn't until we were in the car, and I was trying to fix my face, that I saw it. A golf-ball-size lump that was black and blue under my eye. I gulped but didn't say anything because I didn't want to cause any more fights. I remember just watching a single tear run down my face.

When I arrived home, Nick kissed me goodnight as if nothing had happened. As if he hadn't just slapped me across the face and yelled at me. I remember walking into the house and telling my mum that I had been hit in the face with a soccer ball and that I now had a black eye. She seemed to believe me, well, I think she did. Maybe she didn't, but she didn't say anything. I went into my room and cried myself to sleep, and in that moment, a piece of me died. My hopes and dreams of what real love was, were crushed, and I had taken the position from my mum as the one being abused.

My relationship with Nick continued for another sixteen years and we had two children together. During this time I was physically, emotionally, financially and sexually abused. I don't recall there ever being a day during those sixteen years where I wasn't being abused in some sort of way. There was always some sly comment about my weight, my looks or how I couldn't care for him etc. The only time I actually had some peace was when he was in jail for nine months for hoon driving. I was able to do what I wanted, go where I wanted and even spend more time with my family. He would still call me every night, most times just to see what I was doing, but I always knew what time he was calling so I kinda made sure I was home. Still controlling and abusive, yes, but not like how he usually was.

Whilst Nick was in prison, I made some new girlfriends and decided to go away with them. Whilst away, I found myself. I was carefree, and most importantly, happy. I came home with a new sense for life – or so I thought.

Not long after I got back, Nick was released from jail. Earlier than expected, actually. He called me one night and told me I needed to pick him up from jail at 10am the next day and that he was so excited to be coming home and how much he loved me and the kids. At that moment, the new lease on life I had was suddenly gone. I knew how life was now going to be. Yes, sure, I could have left Nick whilst he was in jail, but I guess I felt sorry for him. He had no family except me, and the kids and I knew it had been hard for him in jail, and I fell back into his trap. Every night he would tell me he loved me and how much he missed me and all the plans he had made for our future.

As reluctant as I was to be with him, I still went to pick him up that morning. There I stood, waiting for the man who had hurt me for so long to come out of the place where I believed he belonged. Nick was so happy he came running down the driveway and burst into tears as he hugged me. A shiver went down my spine knowing this was bullshit, but I hugged him back. We went home and had sex. I had no emotions, nothing, just laid there dreaming that I was somewhere else, like I had done many times before. Nick wanted us to have another baby because he thought everything was perfect between us, but I told him maybe later. No way was I going to have another child with this man.

In the beginning of this 'perfect' new relationship with Nick, things were going great. He was helpful, took care of the kids and the house, and was nice to me. That was all until he started to get into online gambling and methamphetamine. Nick had not had a job since he got out of jail, so I was paying all the bills, buying all the food etc. but he still managed to have money for drugs and gambling. I always wondered where he got it from ... then

I realised it was from me!!! Nick had somehow gotten into my online banking accounts and was transferring money to himself. I never looked at my accounts and just waited for statements.

When I found out, I flew into a rage. I was working full-time and yet he was spending my money. *No way, José!!!* We argued for days and days after I found out, and he just told me that he had always paid for stuff so now it was my turn. *What the fuck???* I had always worked in that relationship, unlike him. During those days of arguing, I realised a leopard can't change its spots no matter how hard it tried to make them stripes. Nick lost thousands and thousands of dollars gambling online. One night alone he lost six thousand dollars. Six thousand dollars of my hard-earned money, at that. Not only was he gambling, but he was doing drugs. It costs 250 dollars for a bag of rock/ice, whatever you want to call it.

Luckily – if you would even call it that – Nick managed to get a job. He was what I called a high-functioning drug addict. He would go to work high. I always hoped I would get a phone call telling me he had been in an accident. Bad thoughts, I know, but when you've been through what I had been going through, you'd have these thoughts too. As much as I would love to tell you things got better after Nick got a job, they didn't. He seemed to be moodier than ever and everything – like, *everything* – I did was wrong. I'll always remember the night he turned to me and said, 'I've been good, haven't I? I haven't hit you … yet.' The way he said that was like I should give him a gold star for not being violent, for not hitting a girl, for not hitting the mother of his children. From that day forward I knew that a punch or a kick was just around the corner, and of course it came a few days later. As the abuse got worse and worse – if that was even possible – I began to lose myself once again, I was depressed. Always sad and angry. Hated everyone. I hated the world, but mostly, I hated myself. I had let myself down. Let my family down and let my children down.

I stayed with Nick for another two years after he was released from prison. It wasn't until I had been held hostage with my children for three days that I needed to finally get out. So, on 26 September 2015, I picked up the phone and made a call to my mum to collect me. It was the hardest thing I have ever had to do in my life. Call my mum and tell her I need her to help me get out. Why was it so hard? My entire life up until that moment, I always did things alone. I never asked for help. I would just work it out myself. But that day, I hid in the upstairs walk-in wardrobe and told my mum she needed to come quickly. She didn't ask any questions and told me she was on her way. I quickly started to pack. My clothes, the kids' clothes, and all our important documentation. Nick must have realised that I had been upstairs for a while when he came storming into the bedroom. He saw the suitcase and began yelling and screaming and telling me that I was not going anywhere and no way in hell were the kids coming with me. I didn't look up from what I was packing. I just kept saying to myself, *It's okay, we're leaving. Mum is on her way.*

Nick didn't like this new attitude that I had so he began to lay into me. One punch, two punches. A kick here and there thrown into the mix. Still, with every punch and kick, I continued to pack. Nothing was more important than that. No matter how much pain or blood that came out of me, I was getting out of there. Yes, I could have stopped packing, but I didn't. I don't know why I didn't. Maybe I thought if I stopped, I wouldn't have left.

After twenty-five minutes, I finally heard my mum yell out my name. I grabbed the suitcase and started to go down the stairs only to have him kick me down them. There I went, down the staircase, with the suitcase fumbling over me. I ran to the door even though I was in pain and opened it up for my mum. She didn't say anything. She just walked inside and said hello to the kids. Nick came down a few moments later, and realising my mum was there, he suddenly turned into this sooky little baby. He began crying to my mum. Started calling her 'Mum' and saying he didn't know why I was doing this to our family and leaving him. My mum was having none of it. She just kept saying, 'I don't know.' We eventually got all the suitcases, toys etc. into the car when Nick locked the gate. We couldn't leave. He demanded I give him two thousand dollars and the car. I was so desperate to leave I just gave in.

'Fine,' I said. I asked my mum if she could drive me but he disagreed. I had to go alone, and my mum and children were to wait with him. I drove as fast as I could to the ATM. I came back, threw the money at him and we were finally on our way out of there. I cried in the car all the way to my sister's house. I don't know what I was actually crying about to be honest, maybe it was happiness, grief, crying for my children, or crying for the little girl I had lost.

The abuse didn't stop after I left Nick. The phone calls and the text messages I received stressed me out so much I ended up in the hospital. The calls and texts finally ended in March 2016 when I had to get a Violent Restraining Order (VRO) on him (but that's a story for another time).

It is now 2021. I haven't seen or heard from Nick since 2017. My children haven't seen him since March 2016. Whilst I know that it has been a while since my children have seen their 'father' I also know the hurt and pain he caused them. Both my children had to do some sort of therapy to help them process what they had been through. They are both amazing, gentle and happy children now, and I don't want anything to jeopardise that. If they choose to see him when they are eighteen, then that is up to them. Also, he hasn't actually reached out or looked for his children.

So, me, how am I? Well, let me tell you, things have been fucking hard, but they also have been amazing. I did meet someone, got married, got divorced, *blah blah blah*, but I'm doing great! I did a lot of therapy to get to where I am now. A lot of hard work. I'm in a much better place than I was when I was with Nick. I am now an advocate against domestic violence. I speak in front of hundreds of people sharing my lived experience and knowledge. I am an ambassador to many brands whose focus is on domestic violence. I am also about to roll out a high school program that will educate the next generation on what an unhealthy, abusive relationship looks like. I truly believe that if I can prevent one girl/woman from going through what I went through, then everything I went through with Nick was worth it.

I am no longer afraid to share my experiences and talk about what happened to me because I am a SURVIVOR!!! With everything I went through during my childhood, with Nick and everything else that has happened to me, I am still here writing these words for you to read *(damn,* I just made myself cry).

So, to anyone out there who may be reading this and is going through the same thing in silence, know you are not alone. Many women out there are going through the same thing as you and they have come out and thrived. I know it's hard, dark and scary because you don't know what's out there, but trust me, it's nothing compared to the nightmare you are living in now. There is a light at the end of the tunnel. Don't get disheartened, or feel shame or embarrassment if you leave then go back. It can take up to seven times to leave for good. One day, you will get out and stay out. Then you will live the life that you deserve. You deserve to live a life, and not just survive. You deserve real love. You deserve happiness. You deserve everything you want.

So, my parting words to you are:
Stay strong. Stay beautiful. I believe you.
Xoxo S

Heartbroken

HEARTBROKEN.

Emma

My sister was the seventy-first girl that died in 2016 from domestic violence. She was stabbed to death in a government building, in a system that was there to serve and protect.

We were best friends from very early on. In our teenage years, we would quarrel over clothes and silly things, like teenagers do. When I had my daughter, my sister was the first person to hold her. We were always there for each other. I was at all her children's births, and we spoke almost daily. She was amazing. And so beautiful. She was well-loved by friends and lit up any room she walked in.

Sarah met Paul on a dating app, and the relationship developed pretty quickly. He basically moved in straight away, and within three months, they were pregnant. He seemed to be a straight-up guy, treated my sister alright and spoke normally to me. My sister was working at a day care centre, and managed to build a house in the suburbs. Once the house was built and they were settled in, it came to light that he wasn't paying the mortgage, the water, the electricity or any other bills because he believed he was a part of the Freemasons. Apparently, a certificate states you are not required to pay taxes to the government and all this other jargon. My sister found out when she came home to a foreclosure sign. They spilt up for a while but eventually made up, moved in together, and she fell pregnant with her second child.

My sister was telling me that Paul didn't take the news of the baby well and started saying things like, 'You've trapped me. You need to get rid of it.' This was confusing to me because they already had a child, so how was that trapping him?

One day, she finally had enough and stayed at my house with her kids. I heard them once on the phone and he was saying really nasty things to her, yelling and screaming. I asked her if he had ever hit her and she insisted he hadn't. I actually answered the phone one time when he called because she just couldn't deal with him anymore. He was raging and I said, 'Hey, cut it out. This is Emma.'

And he said, 'Well put that bitch on the phone.'

I said, 'No, she's had enough of that. She's had enough of you. You can deal with me. What is your problem?' He just hung up.

I was previously in a domestic violence relationship myself, so I could see his behaviour escalating.

I'm an investigator so I gave her tips on being safe. Despite this, he eventually found out where she lived by slipping an old iPhone under the seat of the car when he was putting the kids' bags in during an access visit. He tracked her movements and even found out where I lived.

He lured my sister into the Joondalup Courthouse over a non-existent debt of two thousand dollars. I believe he picked this place because she refused to see him anywhere else. I also think he thought that he would get off and beat the system using a poor mental health argument. He Googled the venue and premeditated the execution. In my heart, I know that if the children had been there, he would have hurt them as well. He wanted Sarah to suffer so he would have made her watch him do it.

We had actually asked if I could accompany her in the courthouse, but they said that wasn't permitted. We explained that she felt frightened and unsafe. They said, 'It's only a simple petty claims thing. There's no need to have anybody here. She'll be well protected.' But she wasn't.

So, Sarah signs into the courthouse and takes a seat and makes eye contact with Paul. They are called into the room by the mediator and he simply asks, 'Sarah, do you owe this money?'

She replies, 'No.'

The mediator then advises Paul that they can't do anything in petty claims court. All parties then agree to take the matter to family court. The meeting is over. The mediator stood up to open the door to let them out. As he stood up to go to the door, Paul stepped over to my sister. He pulls a knife out and cuts my sister six times. Twice in the face, once in the hand as she tries to protect herself, once in the top of the ear, once down the neck and once severing the carotid artery in her throat, causing her to bleed out and die.

The mediator actually thought that Paul was punching my sister and said, 'You can't do that, mate, you need to stop.' Then Paul turns around with the knife in his hand and the mediator puts up his hands to defend himself.

Paul throws the knife down and slides down the wall to the floor. He doesn't run. He sits there and starts to empty out his pockets as if he is preparing to be arrested.

The ambulance arrived within three minutes, but due to the amount of blood loss, she ended up going into cardiac arrest and passed away.

He knew exactly where to cut her because he used his commando training. And what's even more heartbreaking is that he threatened his previous spouse, mother of his eldest son, with the same method of fatality with a knife in her neck.

It turned out there was no security at the courthouse that day as they were in-between companies due to a budget cut.

I had told Sarah to call me as soon as she was done with the meeting. Half an hour had passed so I gave her a call to check on her. She didn't answer because she was fighting for her life. I figured she would call me when she got out so I left it.

My dad called me a few hours later at work in a panic, insisting I come home. I told him I couldn't as I was the only one at work. He wouldn't tell me anything else and just said, 'Emma, come home now.'

I thought something had happened to Nana. I called my boss and he said, 'Just leave. Just leave.'

So I'm driving home and I have this brilliant idea. *Call Adam*, my brother. *Call Adam. He'll know what's happened.* I wish I never did. But I did call him, and he answered. I knew straight away something terrible had happened because he was crying. I said, 'Adam, what's wrong?'

And he replies, 'Just come home. Where are you?'

'Dad's just called me, told me to come home. What's wrong? What's wrong with Nana? You know?'

And he says, 'Nothing's wrong with Nana.' And then he starts to cry and he never cries.

And I say, 'No, you need to tell me what's wrong. Just tell me what's happening.' But he wouldn't tell me. He continued to cry. And I was crying because he was crying, and I said, 'Adam, tell me what's happened, what's happened?'

And Adam said, 'He killed her. He's killed her.'

'What? Sarah?'

'Yeah, he killed her.'

I threw my phone. I nearly crashed my car. I started crying uncontrollably. I managed to pull over in the middle of a bloody busy road, and my boss called, so I found my phone again and answered. He asked if I was alright and I told him my sister had just been murdered. He asked where I was and told me to stay put and he was coming to get me. And I just remember as he pulled me out of the car, I threw up everywhere. And I was so embarrassed because I was sick all over myself. I was just a mess, you know? I don't remember much else. But he put me in the car, and he drove me to my mum and dad.

And that's when it all started. My mum and dad were there with my brothers, police turned up, media turned up. It was like the start of my nightmare because I should have been there for her. But I wasn't. I let her down. And I still believe that even though I know I'm not at fault, I believe I let her down because I wasn't there.

Her children were three and seven when this happened. Trauma officers told us not to lie to them, so they don't find out from somebody else, but don't tell them all the details. We told them Mummy has gone to heaven. Her son kept asking questions and her youngest daughter just stared.

> **PLEASE LEAVE IF YOU ARE SUFFERING FROM DOMESTIC VIOLENCE, IT WILL BE HARD, I KNOW, BUT THE BEST OUTCOME FOR YOU AND/OR YOUR CHILDREN IS BEING SAFE AND FREE FROM THE ABUSE. MATERIAL OBJECTS CAN BE REPLACED BUT LIVES CAN'T BE.**

I said, 'Mummy got hurt and she got so hurt that nobody could fix her. The doctors couldn't fix her. And she had to go to heaven.'

Her son asked, 'What happened to her?'

We said, 'Oh, she got stabbed, she got cut with a knife.'

He asked, 'How?'

I said, 'We don't really know,' because we didn't really know at that stage. We didn't know that her carotid artery had been severed. We just knew that she'd been attacked with a knife.

So he asked, 'Who did it?'

I said, 'Your dad did it.'

'Why?' he asked.

I said, 'I wish I knew.' To this day, I wish I knew why he did it. I don't know why.

I remember her daughter looked at me and said, 'Are you going to be my mum now?' And that killed me. It killed me because she was just a baby, you know?

'No, baby. You only get one mum,' I said, 'but I'll be the best aunty you're going to have ever.'

'Okay,' she said, and that's the only words that she said about it the whole night. Sarah's son was just crying hysterically. Now that he's older, he still holds so much anger towards his dad.

Paul was charged with willful murder. He received twenty-four years. He's entitled to parole, and he could be out on parole in 2042 or 2040. He has since tried to appeal his case but lost the hearing.

We all blame ourselves. I feel like I failed. My family feels like they failed. My brother feels like he failed. He blames himself because he was paying for the family court lawyer because my sister couldn't afford it. And he believes that it's his fault because he got the lawyers involved, and Paul killed her for that.

We all hold our own guilt.

I believe we got some sort of justice, but at the same time they're entitled to a speedy trial. But what about family? You know, what about us? He prolonged this court case for three years before we went to trial, so I believe that families should be entitled to a speedy process and not let him play the system and continually have adjournment after adjournment. I went to every hearing, every process of it. My father and I have attended over sixty appointments over these five years or so.

Paul had such a smug face through the hearings. He would roll his eyes. He did not give two shits. There was no remorse. He was just cold. Even his family showed no remorse or sympathy. Not once did they approach my family to exchange any condolences.

On the day she died, half of me died with her. She was my twin, and we did everything together. It was never going to be the same again. I had to build up my walls and be strong to keep this family together. I had to be strong for my children and now her children as well. And I didn't show it, but it was killing me inside. I just got on with it because I needed to get it done. Yeah, I have moments when I completely fall apart and then I cry in the shower. I cry in the shower with my bottle of wine – that's where I do it. So nobody has to see me cry. On my bad days, that's where I'll be.

If I could save another life out there, this is what I would tell you: Be vigilant, be protected and be safe. Talk to people. Let them know if you're scared. Don't ever go anywhere on your own. If you're worried about your safety, look over your shoulder. Watch for the signs. There are lots of red flags. Trust your gut. Don't say, *Oh, nobody is a good person*. If you notice them changing, their behaviour's escalating, get help, get out. There are so many ways to get help, banks can even help you nowadays with domestic violence. If it's a matter of money or whatever, talk to your friends, your family. There are people out there that will help you – don't become a statistic.

As I mentioned briefly, I too was once a victim of domestic abuse. I've been beaten. Knocked unconscious. I've been raped.

And I saw all the signs, but I fell into the trap and ignored them. I finally found the strength to leave for my daughter and created a safe haven for us. If you can't find the power to do it for yourself, do it for your kids.

HEARTBROKEN.

USED

USED.

Anonymous

It was a typical day after school for sixteen-year-old me. I would catch the latest bus out of school so I could spend more time with my friends. We would gossip and giggle over boys we liked. Then I would catch the bus to the main bus port before a quick stroll through the shopping centre to get some fries from McDonald's. As I was waiting in line one day, I made eye contact with this super sexy *boy* who gave me a smile that made me feel so giddy inside.

'Hey, girl. What you want from the menu? Let me hook you up?'

Literally taking a gulp, I faintly whispered – with a stutter, might I add, 'F-f-f-fries, maybe?'

He was with seven other guys and they were all very friendly and chatty. They had matching swag, baggy pants, FUBU and FILA, fresh Nikes. They were cool. Oozing in coolness. Jeremy walked me to the bus station so I could catch my bus home. He actually caught the bus with me and dropped me off to make sure I was safe. I thought that was so romantic. We traded landline numbers and he called me when he got home. We spoke for hours … and often – every single day.

My parents were super strict. No-boyfriend-until-I'm-twenty-one kind of strict. When he called my phone, he got his sister to ask for me. This went on for about three months until my dad caught me talking to him. I was grounded for a month. I was banned from the shops and had to come straight home after school. Jeremy still met me at the bus port every day, and took the thirteen-minute trip home with me just so we could spend time with each other. We made out in the back seat for twelve of those minutes. He managed to convince me to sneak out of the house one night to go to a party. I was crazy for this guy, so of course, I did.

He picked me up with his friend and said he needed to stop by his house to change his sneakers. He invited me in, turned the TV on for me while I sat on the couch and he went into his room. A couple minutes later, a girl came running out crying with her clothes half off. He soon followed. I asked him who she was and he said, 'Don't trip, babe. That's Junior's girl. They arguing.' I didn't think anything of it at the time – I guess you can say that's when the manipulation started.

I heard his friend's car drive off and I questioned Jeremy about where he was going as I thought we were going to a party. He brushed off my questions and carried me to his room saying, 'Fuck that party, girl. We going to have more fun at home.' He was kissing me and telling me how much he loved me. That he wanted to marry me. I'm the most beautiful girl he had ever seen. He threw me on the bed and started to undress. We had only ever kissed at this point, so I was a little bit nervous about where this was going, but I went with it. This was love, right? And I didn't actually hate it. He was gentle. He was a generous lover and kept asking me if I was okay and if I wanted him to stop. At the end of it, I cried. I don't know why I cried, but I just started crying. I asked him to take me home, so we caught a taxi together and I snuck back into my room and cried myself to sleep.

The next day when I saw him at the bus stop, he was acting

a little stand-offish. I asked him if I did something wrong and he totally flipped his attitude and became overly loving and sweet again. Except this time, he didn't catch the bus home with me. I felt gross. I felt that he had finally got what he wanted and now I repulsed him. He rang me that night and my dad answered. You guessed it – I was grounded for another month! I had a massive fight with my dad. I told him I hated him. I never wanted to talk to him again. Everything an angry teenager would say. My mum tried to calm him down but that just made them get into an argument instead. I ran away that night, straight to my boyfriend's house. I found out later that he rang my house because he knew it would piss my dad off and get me in trouble.

Now, Jeremy didn't know I was coming, and he was a little frazzled when I got there. He was sweating. There was a group of girls there and his friends from the mall. It was a weird ambience but again, I just ignored it. He told me to go straight to his room. I sat there for about twenty minutes before he came in. He was pissed. He punched the wall and started throwing his stuff around. I asked him what was wrong. He ignored me and continued swearing and rummaging through things. He left the room and ordered me not to come out. The smashing continued outside, and one girl started screaming, 'STOP! STOP!' I was petrified but also curious so I went to investigate.

Jeremy was beating up this girl saying, 'Where is it? Where is it?' He was looking for some drugs that he was accusing her of stealing. I tried to interrupt but he ordered me back to the bedroom. I tried to leave his house but he dragged me back in by my hair and threw me into his room. I was in shock. I didn't know what to do. I wanted my dad. I felt safe with him. I sat on the bed, lifeless and crying. Jeremy eventually came back in calm and apologised. He started to kiss me and said he didn't mean to, he was just pissed about that thief. He began to undress me and started to have sex with me. I just laid there lifeless. He finished and walked out of the room to order pizza.

I was still lying lifeless on the bed when he came in and said, 'I'm going to have a shower. My wallet's there if the pizza guy comes.' The pizza guy did come and so did a discovery I was not ready for. I quickly glimpsed the driver's licence in his wallet. According to this government-issued card, this guy was sixteen years my senior. He told me he was eighteen! After his shower he was in a much better mood, and I didn't want to rock the boat so I didn't question him about his age.

I stayed at his house for four days without contacting my parents. I felt that I should probably go home as they would be worried. He sweet-talked me out of it, begging me to stay. He bought me gifts. He showered me with praises. Told me he loved me every other hour. I was so in love. Nothing else mattered.

Three months passed. I stopped going to school to hang with my boyfriend every day, do drugs and have sex. I completely lost myself and any dreams I had for my future. I bumped into my parents at the shop and they saw me making out with Jeremy. My dad was heartbroken. He started crying and begged me to come back home. Jeremy told him to fuck off. I was so out of it it's still kind of a blur, but I do remember being prompted to say that I was happy and not to worry about me because Jeremy was looking after me. My dad refused to take no for an answer and attempted to carry my frail body away. Jeremy flipped to angry mode and started beating up my father. Security had to break them up and we got kicked out. I was so numb. I was emotionless.

My dad begged me again and in frustration he yelled, 'What's so special about this black cunt? I'm your father!'

I guess it was my groomed and doped-up mind that barked

back at him saying, 'Fuck you, I love him. We're getting married. Leave us alone. I hope you die.'

Two weeks later, my parents died in fatal car crash.

I WAS BROKEN. I AM BROKEN STILL. I said the most disgusting thing to my parents, and it was the last thing I said to them. What's worse is that my dad's last memory of me is at the lowest point in my life.

From there, EVERYTHING escalated. Jeremy had his friend Robby come over with some 'off-the-truck' branded merchandise. He tried to make me feel better by showering me with gifts. It felt good to be spoilt. I felt special. He asked me to pick whatever I liked. I chose a couple of items and Jeremy asked what the total price was. His friend said, 'Eleven Gs.' Money was never an issue with Jeremy. He was a street pharmacist, so cash was always around. But this time, he was hesitant.

'Yo, my dude. That's a stretch. I don't have that kind of money.'

The guy selling the goods looked me up and down and said, 'Maybe we can arrange something else.'

I laughed it off as a joke but no-one else was laughing with me. I replied with a stern, 'Hell no, you are joking – right?' But they weren't.

Jeremy said, 'I'm cool with it, babe. It will be fun for you, and you get your bags and shit. You've been wanting that bag for a while, spoil yourself. It's Robby, he's the homie.' Jeremy stood up, shook Robby's hand and said, 'I'll give you guys some space.'

Robby was smooth with his

> **IF YOU ARE LUCKY ENOUGH TO HAVE FAMILY TRYING TO HELP YOU, DON'T PUSH THEM AWAY. THEY ARE HELPING BECAUSE THEY LOVE YOU.**

approach. It was an eerie deja vu moment of the first time I had sex with Jeremy. I came to find out later that this was their play. They would shower girls with kindness and gifts only to abuse them and pimp them out once they were under their control. By the end of the week, I had slept with six of his friends because 'they all heard how good I was'. I didn't fight it. I just laid there lifeless.

Jeremy started feeding me stronger drugs to make sure I was completely weak and started to pimp me out. I was being raped up to four times a day. I didn't even feel anything anymore. Nothing physical. Nothing emotional. I was dead to the world. The saddest part is whenever I was having sex with all these men, I let my imagination take me to a happy place.

It was always the same scene. I was six and my dad was chasing me around the backyard. He would pretend to be a dinosaur and chase me with his roar. When he caught me, he would tickle me and shower me with kisses. He would say, 'Who loves you? Who loves you?'

And he wouldn't stop until I said, 'Daddy loves me.' He promised me from a very young age that he would always protect me. And he tried, but I didn't let him.

I didn't have anywhere to go as my parents were gone. I had no family. I pushed all my friends away, so it made no sense to run away. At least I had a bed and knew where I was getting my next hit from.

One day, Jeremy told me I was moving in with a client for a month. I lost my shit. I didn't want to be with anyone else. I felt safe with Jeremy. He took off his belt and started whipping me. Across my body. Across my face. He wouldn't stop until I agreed.

When his client came to pick me up, Jeremy whispered in my ear, 'Who loves you?' This sick fuck knew that was a cherished moment with my dad and he used it to break me. I thought I was already in hell, but I was in paradise in comparison. My temporary pimp had me having sex with up to eight guys a night. And he refused to give me drugs. He wanted his girls clean. I was in the house with four other girls. We had a room each which we weren't allowed to leave without permission. The mattress was on the floor and the window was blacked out and barred. I became such an angry person as I was sober and deep in my thoughts. I would fight my pimp, fight my clients, who would in turn rough me up and hold me down. Do whatever they wanted with my body and leave me for dead. I fell pregnant. Jeremy found out and came to collect me straight away. He called me a whore and beat me until I had a miscarriage. I bled heavily on a client so I was given a break from working. However, I fell really sick and had an infection because I didn't pass all of the placenta. I had a seizure and woke up in the hospital.

They told me I was dropped off at the front and they had no idea who I was. I told them everything. The police came and questioned me for hours. I was eventually discharged, and I was rehomed at a women's refuge. I stayed there for a year and got my life back together. It took me a very long time to trust men again as I knew no-one could ever match up to my Dado.

I am married now to the most gentle soul and four months pregnant with our first child. It's a girl. I'm terrified that she may live the same fate as me. My parents did everything right except that they were far too strict with me and weren't open with communication. I was scared of them. It made me rebel. This is a lesson I have learnt and will be mindful of with my daughter. I am at peace with my past, but I am still regretful every day for how I treated my parents. This is something I could only fully understand now that I'm about to be a parent myself. You know in your heart that you would do absolutely anything to protect them. I am still in therapy, and I've found hypnosis and psychotherapy work best for me and my situation. As for him, I heard he's in jail and I hope he rots in there.

If you're reading this, I want you to remember that you mean the world to someone, so if they are trying to help you, then let them – please.

Dado and Mama, I miss you so much and I'm so sorry for letting you down. I hope you are looking down on me and I'm making you proud. You're going to be grandparents soon, please watch over her and protect her. I love you and I wish I could hug you both one last time.

jealous

JEALOUS.

Anonymous

I never considered myself a jealous person. I was in the popular groups in school and had a bunch of friends. I was invited to all the parties and events. After completing my uni degree, I received a job placement in my dream job as a HR manager for a recruitment agency. The excitement lasted about three hours after my first encounter with Jessica. Busty and blonde Jessica. The office It girl. Being new, I made it my mission to befriend everyone in my department. I found out very quickly that the HR girls were very cliquey. I put my hand out to introduce myself to Jessica and she looked me up and down and said, 'Gross,' and pranced off. I was mortified, I had never been rejected before.

The bullying continued and my issue was that staffing complaints are made *to* the HR department, but the abuse was coming *from* the HR department. My confidence quickly spiralled downwards and I found myself becoming a really toxic and negative person. I would waste my weekends away getting drunk and sleeping with a different guy every other week. One of my girlfriends pulled me aside and pleaded with me to get my life under control.

So I did. I went to work during the week, kept my head down and spent weekends with supportive friends. It was at a house party that I was introduced to my Prince Charming. He was tall, with blue eyes, mousey blond hair and a bright white smile you could see from the moon. He was charismatic, the life of the party and he was paying attention to me. We got to talking and laughing, lots of laughing. I haven't felt this good since high school.

James romanced the hell out of me. He took me to dinners, visited me at work, sent me flowers, you name it. I didn't sleep with him until we had been dating for over six months. I felt so connected to him, I didn't need to. I felt sexy and confident again.

But – and there's always going to be a but, right?! One day at work I caught a group of the catty bitches stalking James' profile on Facebook. I saw red. I confronted them and they laughed my questioning off. By this stage I was living with James and when I got home that night, I began to see red again. I didn't get any answers from the girls so I started to question him. This was our first fight. Jessica walked past me the next day at work and snickered, 'Say hi to James for me.' Something flicked a switch in me after that because I started to question all of his movements. I would constantly check his phone, his emails, his Facebook messages etc. I never found anything but that didn't stop me. I found a reason to accuse him and argue about anything. I think I ended up smashing at least eight of his mobile phones, two laptops and three PlayStations during episodes of rage.

One night he was at his best friend's bucks party and he wasn't replying to my messages. I rang and it went straight to voicemail. I rang all his friends, about ten times each like a psycho but no reply. I swear if they weren't on a pub crawl I would have been at the venue within five minutes, I just didn't know where to find them. I stayed up waiting for him and he finally arrived at 4:37am. I yelled. I swore. I threw things. But this time was different. This was the first time I actually struck him. With my home-alone-safety baseball bat, to be precise. He blocked all my hits and that made me even madder. He took the bat out of my hands and walked away. He never fought back. I ran up behind him and hit him in the back of the head with a book that was on the shelf next to him. Again. He didn't fight back and just went to bed. I had no idea what had gotten into me. I slept it off in the TV room alone that night.

Gradually, I banned him from going out with the boys. I didn't allow him to visit any friends, and his friends were only allowed to visit if I was home. He went straight to work and home again, I made sure he didn't make any unknown stops. If he wanted to go to the shops, I had to come. His parents' house was absolutely off the table as they hated me and would only try to turn him against me. We hung with my friends and my family only. My insecurities made him feel belittled, even though he was physically much bigger than me. I noticed on his bank statement there was a charge instore at David Jones. I had not been to this department store with him so when I asked him about it, he told me that he went there when he finished work early one day. We were at the dinner table and I saw red again. I snapped and stabbed his arm with my steak knife ... a few times. That night I made him email his work to arrange for his future wages to be paid into my account and I would distribute an allowance to him after he paid the household bills.

He tried to leave a few times but I would threaten him with suicide until he eventually called my bluff. I emailed him a photo of a concoction of pills and said, *This is your fault.* I woke up in the hospital and they had pumped my stomach. I was on suicide watch and the nurse had asked James to watch over me. He felt so guilty and promised to never leave my side again. He stuck by more threats, more tantrums, more physical abuse and all the bullshit I put him through. I'm so embarrassed for all of it. Not to make an excuse for it, but when I saw red, it felt like I spaced out and had no control of what I was doing. I don't even remember doing the things I did until I snapped out of it. James was honestly too kind for this earth. Definitely too kind for me. Through all the fucked up shit I did, he never raised his voice or hands once. He didn't even flinch when I hurt him, he was my human punching bag. I'm ashamed to say that's how I trained him to be. He learnt that if he tried to stop me I would get more uncontrollably violent, so he preferred to cop it and move on with the night.

His friends and family constantly tried to intervene when they saw bruises and cuts, but I had fallen pregnant so he felt even more obligated to stay in this situation. We eloped. I was a horrible person. A very bitter person and I don't even know why I did all those things. When our daughter turned two, a new lady started at his work and they built a friendship quite quickly. He kept this a secret from me. She became his confidant. He told her everything about the home situation, his finances and my insane list of forbidden activities. He went to work one day with a black eye, scratches on his neck and cheek. She convinced him to see a counsellor about what was going on at home. He took her advice and saw one during work hours. He didn't have any money to pay so she would pay for the sessions for him.

Over a three-month period, I started to notice a slight change in him. When I started a fight, he would slowly start to stick up for himself. If I hit him he would block me or just walk out the house. He started getting payments back into his own account again. I felt like I was losing control and I hated it. I threatened him with suicide again and he said, 'Maybe that would be the best thing for Macy [my daughter] and I.' It was then that I knew I had lost him. He started to invite his friends and family over. I would make a scene every time. I was no longer hiding it and would attempt to attack him in front of them. I was on a dark mission to regain control so I put a tracking device on his car. He was leaving work each Tuesday to go to an address for one hour every week. I had convinced myself it was a prostitute or side girlfriend. I found out the hard way that it was his counselling sessions. I rocked up to the clinic on a Tuesday as he does and snuck in through the back door trying to catch him in the act.

I found him in a room with a male counsellor, holding a box of tissues with a puffy face from crying. The worst part is that I didn't even feel bad. I was mad that I was wrong. His counsellor invited me to take a seat and offered to hear my side of the story. I refused to talk and began to walk out the room when James grabbed my arm, fell to his knees and said, 'Please. I'm begging you. I need help. I don't see any purpose in living anymore.' Suddenly I felt something weird. I felt empathy towards him. I sat down but I didn't say a word. The counsellor and James were pointing their finger at me and blaming me for everything, which of course I denied and threw the blame on James. I didn't stay the whole session as I was over being thrown under the bus. When James came home, I ignored him. In fact, we didn't speak for over a year besides the meaningless, *Put the bin out. Macy needs a nappy change. Dinner's ready.* And to be honest, I didn't feel any way about it.

We were living together, in separate rooms and in completely separate worlds. I stayed focused on my career and he would his. My mum had Macy for most of the time as I worked so often. James would pick her up after he had finished work and I would go down to the pub to hook up with guys. He didn't know any of this and I don't know if he was doing the same as I stopped looking through his stuff. I can only assume he didn't because he would come home straight after work to be with the baby. On my birthday, which ended our ignoring-each-other period, I came home from the pub to a bunch of flowers and a present all wrapped up.

I had basically just fucked a random tattoo-sleeved guy in the bathroom of the pub while my husband was at home with our daughter bearing gifts, even though I had been such a horrible bitch over the last six years. I crumbled. I fell to the floor and cried. Sobbed. Hysterically. Loud enough that he came rushing out of bed thinking I was hurt. He checked my body to see if I was injured as no words were coming out my mouth.

> **DON'T LET JEALOUSY GET THE BETTER OF YOU.**

He hugged me. He held me tight. He embraced me. We sat on the floor not talking for about an hour until I fell asleep. He carried me into my bed and I blurted out, 'I'm sorry!' I started crying, then he started crying. That was the first time I had ever acknowledged my wrongdoing. That was the first time in years that we weren't arguing. He kissed me. I felt loved again. We made love. It was the most magical and sensual sex we had ever had. He touched me softly. Kissed me everywhere. Looked me deep in my eyes as he thrusted in and out of me with his perfect penis. It was like the switch had flicked back again and I was no longer evil. A prince's kiss saved me.

The next day, everything went back to normal. We were a happy family for once. Macy was a little taken aback as she was used to the divide, but it was a change she welcomed. We enrolled into couples therapy and I also started seeing a therapist independently. I found out I was pregnant again but a dark cloud loomed over me as I didn't know who the father was. James and I had finally gotten back to a healthy space. I was working hard on my own issues. I quit my job and was no longer working in that toxic environment. I couldn't find it in my heart to break his heart. Imagine me having a heart and some feelings, hey?!

When my son was born, I was diagnosed with postnatal

psychosis. I lost sense of all reality and withdrew from my happiness again. I was admitted into a ward as I was convinced James was trying to kill me and my son. They let my son stay in the hospital with me, but I couldn't be alone with him. And because of my past attempts, I was put on suicide watch.

It took me a good six months to get back to *normal* and James stayed by my side for the whole ordeal. After everything I have put him through, how did I get so lucky to have him? Every day, it eats me up that I did those fucked up things, and I'm learning to forgive myself as James has already forgiven me. My mum is Latino and she believes I was cursed by a jealous girl. Call it a cop-out but I can see it having some truth to it.

I don't know how to make up for what I did. I acknowledge that I was a horrible person who did unthinkable things. I have learnt from my mistakes and try to better myself every day – for James, my kids and myself. The biggest takeaway from my experience is that it's more beneficial to talk to a therapist than to make up stories in your head. Once paranoia kicks in, it's a hard demon to let go of. If I had gotten help from the start for my insecurities, I wouldn't have hurt James. If I had accepted help when my son was born, I wouldn't have had to leave my children. If I had listened to our friends begging me to seek help, I wouldn't have abused my body. There are so many ifs to factor in but the biggest one is if James had decided to leave me, I don't think I would still be here, writing my story. I owe him so much more than an apology. I owe him for saving my life, giving me endless chances and for giving me two beautiful children (both kids look like me so I'm sticking with it).

dominated

DOMINATED.

Dominique

My name is Dominique and I met my abuser, who is now my estranged husband, when I was seventeen. I am thirty-four years old now and have been away from the abuse for only four months. I endured sixteen years of it; some physical and financial, but mainly severe emotional abuse and manipulation. My story, like many I am sure, is about how much I tolerated from him for so long because I never thought I could leave, and how hard he made it to escape. But I did it!

When I met him I was recovering from a stroke, I was in intensive therapy for this and very vulnerable. He was six years older, very charming and very persistent about having me. At the time, I thought it was very flattering that he wanted to spend every day with me, introduce me to his circle of friends, and shower me with attention and gifts. Before I knew it, I was consumed by the relationship. It became serious quickly. He moved in with me when I was nineteen, and we were married by twenty-one.

I was a bright, happy child and an outgoing teen, but by the time I was married, I barely saw my own friends because he disapproved of them. I was surrounded by his circle of other controlling males and their wives or partners. I'd been moulded to listen to him from a young age and now I was becoming the wife he wanted. Whenever I lashed out about how I really felt, or wanted to do something without him, I was automatically shut down harshly till I stopped asking. Already he controlled me and manipulated every situation in my life. This was just the beginning.

In the initial years, before having kids, there were a few pushes and shoves and a lot of standing over me, but no major physical assaults – until February 2011. We were at a nightclub celebrating his friend's partner's birthday (surprise – *his* group). He wanted to leave and I wanted to stay but we were already out and I was following him. We argued because I almost never got to go out. The arguing escalated and he grabbed me. He is very tall and strong and I am only 153cm tall and petite. I retaliated, then he grabbed my hair and was forceful. People on the street noticed. Then the bouncers ran over and started fighting with him. Police were called and he assaulted them too, and was arrested that night. For my safety the police issued a Violence Restraining Order (VRO) against him.

After the incident I was brought home by his uncle and friends, and told to try to speak to police to have the VRO dropped. The order said he wasn't allowed at the house. The police came to my house and he was there, though I told them he wasn't. They told me to be careful as he was dangerous, and that the VRO would protect me for my own safety. I was distraught by this. I was crying. Truth hurts!

I was taken to court by my husband's close friend (a criminal lawyer) for the court hearing and made to underplay the incident. I was told to deny that the events were an ongoing trait, and that they were out of character (I became so good at doing this over the next decade). However, they were very much in character. The VRO was dropped. My husband had made me feel like the incident that night was my fault and so did everyone around him.

I began, somehow, to believe this was the case, even though I also knew it was wrong.

When I became pregnant with our first child a couple of months after this event, I was so excited about growing my sweet little angel. Little did I realise that this would ultimately lead to him to having full control of me, and taking even my limited amount of freedom, at that time, away. Even the first night in hospital he said he was going home to feed the dogs, and would be back in the morning. He went out to a club instead. My best friend, who I had been estranged from at the time due to his disapproval, had seen him. He told her not to tell me. She came to the hospital the next morning and he was forced to tell me. He didn't stay long that day, recovering from his big night out. This behaviour would sum up most weekends over the next decade. Now I had a baby and I would be at home looking after him, which allowed my husband to control the situation even more completely. My view was that he could do what he wanted, but this baby was the centre of my life. He coldly used this to emotionally manipulate and control me for the rest of our marriage.

I was working two days a week after my son was born, and I became very close with the staff at my workplace. I loved going to work. It was the only time I got to be me again. Every other day I was Mummy to my son, and slave to my husband. In 2013 I became pregnant with my second child. My toddler had stopped napping now and was so full of energy, and I was tired – so tired. My relationship with my husband got really rocky, and I didn't put up with as much. He was going out a lot and I assume on drugs (he had been a user at varying levels throughout our relationship) because he was staying up through the night until early morning. I was always so alone, trying to deal with it all. One time I had got annoyed he hadn't answered the phone all night (a very common occurrence), and I was scared and having bad pains, and when he got home he pushed me. I remember looking up from the floor while he screamed at me, telling me to abort our baby. He soon hired an office above a club and for the remainder of the pregnancy he was out a lot, and I got on with my life as much as possible.

Our second child was born in 2014. Another perfect little human. He made it easier for me to be distracted by my marriage issues. My husband then got a factory for work, in which he spent a lot of nights. I later found out it was mostly used for 'the boys' to hang out, drink, do drugs, and from stories I heard, probably other women. Looking back, I don't know how I couldn't see what was going on, but I had a new baby and a toddler, and a heart that believes the best in people.

He had me sheltered my whole adult life, resulting in me having such a naive perspective on the world around me. My world was his world. The only acceptable friends were the wives of his friends, and we mainly did things with his family. When I was with my own family he would constantly phone or start a fight with me while I was with them. I would see my old friends only a couple of times a year (literally). Even then, I would have so much anxiety getting up the courage to tell him because he would go off his head about 'how much he hates them'. To avoid the conflict I used to not tell him if I could avoid it, and pretend I ran into them accidentally. If he knew, he would call me every two minutes about the most minor things. It was a joke, but a very sick one!

I had one work friend that he accepted. She was single but not a party girl. She didn't push me to go out. She would come to our house and not ask me to hers, so this suited him and he allowed the friendship to continue. She always agreed with him and told him what he wanted to hear. She knew I was in a bad marriage and was even witness to assaults, but we both knew he was never going to let me leave easily. So she just helped make my time at home better for me. She was there most weekends to keep me company when he was out. He was happy I was distracted from what he was doing. She was invited to family events such as Easter.

One Easter he got really nasty. I answered back. He had picked up my eldest, who would have been about three at the time. I went to get him and take him upstairs because I had had enough. He pushed me so hard I flew across the room into the door. I hit it so hard a picture fell off the wall and smashed. I was hysterical, my friend grabbed my son from him, took him upstairs and I called his parents. He was spoken to by them. However, he was so angry at me for telling his family: 'How dare you expose my behaviour?' As always I'm sure I apologised for causing it all.

Not too much longer after the previous assault, he insisted I needed to leave my job and help him with his business. This was the next stage of his control. I lost all control of my life after this, and the only financial stability we had. It also gave him an excuse to blame even more things on me, and I was now constantly reminded that he brought in the money and I had no value.

He spent money like there was no tomorrow, and this behaviour put us into hardship constantly. He felt he deserved everything and I never had a say. He bought expensive toys and gadgets for himself instead of paying bills, but when he was stressed about bills he blamed it on me. I would always ask my parents for money to get us through and keep food on our table. He never went without, though; always a budget for cigarettes, going out and drinking. He constantly withdrew cash from accounts. He would lie and make up excuses. I would later find out this was to support his drug use.

In 2017 he was charged with cocaine possession. He went to court and was convicted. I had no idea any of this happened. It was all hidden from me. To explain some of the spending, he would constantly tell me his brother was in trouble and needed to pay people. To cover up, he then isolated me from his brother so I didn't question him. All to cover up his habit and his reckless and selfish use of our money.

Our marriage, I knew, was in decline. I was starting to really feel it but I knew I could never leave. He often told me, 'The only way you will leave is in a body bag,' and I wasn't strong enough to go up against him with two little kids who needed me – and he knew that. I used to speak with one of the other wives about how unhappy I was, and she could relate since our husbands were constantly together. We would often text each other in the middle of the night, asking if the other had heard from 'our boys'. They never answered their phones and it was the same crap all the time. I cried myself to sleep endlessly wondering what I had done to deserve this life. How could anyone treat someone they say they love, so badly?

I would always say I was done, but I knew I couldn't leave. The feeling of hopelessness used to overwhelm me. At the end of 2019, I finally started talking to my old work friend and opened up about how unhappy I was. It was the end of year, and it was getting harder to keep it to myself because he was home on holidays. That meant more being ordering around by him, more arguments, and no freedom at all during the day. I spent most of my time explaining myself and walking on eggshells. Walking the dog was my only outlet. He did very little with the kids or me for most of those holidays.

I remember 8 January 2020 as the start of the next phase. I had been begging for a couple of days to be taken out. It had been so long. This night, he said to me he was going out with the boys. I was so mad I screamed at him, and he threw me to the couch and got right into my face. His size and his air of aggressiveness was so intimidating. I lashed out and I remember scratching his face to get it away from mine. He then proceeded to throw me around the house. I had had enough. My children were upstairs. I screamed for them to stay there, as they didn't need to see what he was doing. He held me up against the wall with a knife, then backed off but came back with it again. I still remember it as clear as crystal. There was no soul left in his eyes as he held the knife up at me. I was understandably hysterical.

He called my mum and told her I was crazy. Manipulators love to throw the crazy card at you, so they have no accountability for their actions. They turn it onto you because 'you started it' for voicing your feelings (he was so persuasive that I believed it sometimes). My mum came to our house and I told her I had enough. I told her about the knife and his reaction to her was, 'I should have stabbed her.' He then left to go out. He didn't speak to me for a couple days. Remember, it's my fault I need to be punished! He went away with the kids for a couple of nights after this.

I started to talk with a guy. It was harmless and I already knew him, but now I needed a friend and I needed to feel some kind of attention as a woman since I had become nothing to my husband. We only spoke occasionally and it never escalated.

Then COVID-19 hit, and my husband was openly using drugs now. I would see his close friends all drop their phones at his office and go off to the shed. They would all emerge sniffling. Things were deteriorating fast. It was so hard having him around all the time (remember, this was the time of lockdowns). I was in hell. He was

> **I FINALLY MADE IT OUT. I AM IN CHARGE OF MY OWN FUTURE NOW. HE NO LONGER OWNS ME.**

nasty all the time and did nothing. I started sleeping in the spare room. One day I went on a walk with one of the other wives and I mentioned to her how miserable I was, and that I wanted to leave. Her husband (his friend) called me the next day. I told him I had enough, and he said he would bring my husband over to his house and talk to him for me. My husband came home from that conversation not with any new understanding, but with intense anger with me for talking. I was warned not to talk again because I embarrassed him: 'How dare you?' He now knew clearly I wanted to leave the marriage but that was not an option he would consider.

I knew my circle of friends was not safe to talk to about this. I had added a random guy through Instagram. We started chatting and I started talking to him about my home situation. It was pretty harmless but I knew a stranger was safer to talk to than my so-called friends. My husband had always said cheating would be a deal-breaker and deep down I was hoping it would make him leave me if I got caught. On 25 June he wanted my phone to add an app. He went to look into something I had posted and I took the phone from him. He overpowered me and took the phone. He called my mum to shame me and attempted to get *her* to further control me. This didn't work, so I opened up and told her I was talking to someone. I told him again that I wanted to leave. I had been telling him all year but he dismissed it. Instead of helping do his dirty work, my mum backed me up. Once she heard the details she told him how badly he was treating me, how controlling he was, and how she barely knew who I was anymore.

He then changed strategies, but still with the same aims of control. He said he didn't realise how bad it had got, to lead me to do this. He told me I was going to hurt my kids by leaving. He manipulated me with guilt into not leaving that day. This was the worst decision I made. The next nine months of my life consisted of constant abuse and torture. I was in fear for my life every day I endured. It nearly led me to take my own life (if he didn't take it first).

I got a job in July which was my saviour, I was physically safe at those times. I was always scared at home and I never knew what to expect. His control intensified. He removed my social media and wanted access to my phone at all times in the house. He was tracking my every move (literally) and had my phone monitored with software. Yes, he bugged my phone. To cover this up he created an elaborate fantasy. He phoned me one time with, 'I don't want people to call me but they keep telling me what you are doing and who you are with,' (lies, lies, lies). One of his major tactics was to keep me always on edge and fearful. He was reciting phone calls I was having; both my words and the other person's. He made recordings of me at home, sent them to my parents, and replayed them for me. I was physically assaulted on numerous occasions, mentally abused all through the day from first thing in the morning till late at night. Then he used to wake me all though the night screaming at me or obsessing that I talked to a guy. He could not let it go. I kept telling him I *wanted out,* but he wasn't allowing it. He isolated everyone from us and kept taking us on family trips so there was no outside influence. He told me that everyone hated me and that I had lost my mind.

By November, the arguments were constant and I was barley sleeping because of him waking me. I contemplated suicide. The trauma I was enduring every day had broken me, and I had nothing left in me to fight. I knew I had reached my limit and it became apparent that I had a few choices here. I could wait until he killed me (and I know he would have), I could do it myself, or I could reach out and talk. I spoke out to friends, my parents, work colleagues, I saw a counsellor and then I said to him that it was officially over, and went to stay with my parents. This was short-lived this time though.

After a bit over a week, I was manipulated into moving back into the house. He wanted us to try living under the same roof for the kids, but separated. I slept in the kids' beds and I never went back into my bed. He made me sleep with him and then called me a slut and a whore afterwards. After listening to my phone recordings he found out I had slept with someone else when I moved to my mum's. He played it back to me over and over again. The day he found out, he arranged that night for my mum to have the children. I came home from work. He was so high. I said again, 'We are over, I did nothing wrong and I want to go to bed and sleep.' All through that night he continuously woke me. He smashed the door down and threw things at me, and made a huge hole in our kids' room. He hid the car keys and took my phone. He came in and out screaming, and then he would lie down and try to cuddle me. I just stayed quiet that night. I had never been so terrified. I wouldn't leave alive. He was a maniac. He finally passed out the next morning. By this point his drug use escalated (now daily), and so did his associated paranoia. His moods changed so rapidly.

Then the gaslighting intensified. He told his mum, one of his friends who I used to confide in and his lawyer/friend that I was 'in a bad way'. They were all telling me I needed help and that I needed to try to stay and make it work. They were all telling me I was crazy, and that something was wrong with me. It even got to the point when his friend (the lawyer) had made phone calls to get me into a psychiatric hospital to get me help because 'I was not right'. He even had an Uber driver send valium in an envelope for me, to put me to sleep prior to going there the next morning.

My husband said he was going out for a few hours that night. I was on the phone to a guy nervous about what they were trying to get me to do. He came running back. He knew what I was saying and snatched the phone from me. Then the arguing started. He was screaming at me so much that I couldn't cope. I punched a glass frame in front of me and cut my hand.

He called my parents and they spoke to a helpline who advised that the police attend. The police spoke to me while he hovered to watch what I would say. They had to speak to me in the ambulance to get me alone, and then I went to hospital to treat my cuts. The police asked him to leave and said that I would go back to my house after medical treatment. I returned home and he was back again the next morning screaming at me as soon as I woke. He refused to leave our house and I didn't feel safe being in there unprotected anymore. Home felt like jail. He had a huge alarm system installed in the following few days. He finally told me that it was my choice to leave. I knew if I wanted to leave I needed to go, and leave everything I owned, to be free and safe from the torture. The next day I packed my bags and moved to my parents.

However, it still wasn't over. Even after I moved out to my parents' place he started texting me as soon as I woke, and all through the day till late at night, manipulating my emotions and making me fearful every hour of every day. I was physically safe but I woke every night in sweats, scared about where I was. During this period, I was even strangled outside a hotel room in one of his drug rages where he told me how 'easily he would kill me'. I called the police that night but was talked to by his friend to not press charges at the time, and by the time I did, the evidence on cameras was no longer there.

The mental manipulation and abuse continued until March 2021. I got the courage to get a VRO against him. The police were supportive and explained his behaviour was in the 'most dangerous' category. I wish I had done this earlier, but I'm still so happy I made that decision eventually.

Things immediately started to change for the better. I could think for myself again without being coerced. I began to know there was a chance to be happy again and I could control my own life for the first time, a day at a time. I can't even explain enough how life-changing this was for me.

It is now July 2021 and I have never been stronger. I no longer fear every morning. I no longer have to listen to his constant abuse and manipulation, and my life is not in constant risk. I am free and I am starting a new healthy life. I love being a single mum. I will show my boys the strength a woman can have and teach them the respect women like us deserve. I never thought I would leave alive but I am thankful to be here now writing my truth. I am blessed to wake up every morning away from him. There are still scars, I still have so much to overcome, but I am *me* again and I have really amazing friends and family that have stuck by me to help me be here today, and who support me. Most of all I have two beautiful boys who make these wounds worth having.

Over the past sixteen years, I endured emotional, physical and financial abuse. I often ask what I did to deserve all this pain and suffering, but it did bring me two beautiful boys. The guilt doesn't lay on me anymore. I am not a victim but a survivor. He chose to treat me this way and he made me too weak to fight it for so long. I have started a new chapter in my own life now, and I have the chance for a new start. I still have ongoing legal issues to finalise custody and divorce issues but this will eventually pass.

I finally made it out. I am in charge of my own future now he no longer owns me.

trapped

TRAPPED.
Cathy

'Why are you hitting me?' I moaned, as I regained consciousness to discover my partner John squaring-up to punch me in the head again. I was sitting on the toilet and feeling really disoriented, confused and in pain. My clothes were all soaking wet and the floor was covered in vomit.

'You overdosed' he said, 'I'm hitting you to keep you from passing out again. I put you in the shower but that wasn't working.' Turns out that John's little joke towards me had backfired. The last memory I had before this moment was of him passing me a drink at the function centre where his underworld mafia associates had invited us to someone's birthday party. I did not know that the drink was spiked with some drug that John thought would be funny to give me.

I had almost forgotten about this memory until recently. When you have experienced domestic abuse, there are so many moments which are hard to comprehend. Sometimes it is just too difficult to process the horror of the violence at the time it is being inflicted upon us, so our brains learn to compartmentalise and shelve the painful memories away in the deep recesses of our psyche. I have been asking myself how I could forget about having my drink spiked, overdosing and being physically assaulted, and the sad truth is that it is because that moment pales into insignificance compared to many other moments of violence which I have experienced throughout my two long-term abusive relationships.

As a little girl growing up in a loving family on a beautiful farm near Ballarat, I could never have imagined the trauma, pain and abuse which has defined my adult life thus far. When I played with my dolls out in the sunshine, all I could see was a life of possibility lying ahead of me, where I would one day achieve the traditional white picket fence dream of being happily married with children and enjoying success in a career path I had achieved a degree for. At the age of forty-two, as I reflect on all that has happened since I left the safe cocoon of my sheltered country life, I see that the way life has evolved for me is worlds apart from my childhood daydreams.

I was twenty-two when I entered my first abusive relationship with a guy who had grown up in a country town near my family's farm. Our fathers had even spent some time working for the same organisation. This young guy just seemed so utterly normal and typical of the type of men I had grown up around my entire life. I had no initial reason to fear John, but he ended up being responsible for creating hell on earth for

> **ANYONE CAN FALL VICTIM TO PREDATORS LIKE THIS BECAUSE THAT'S JUST THE NATURE OF HOW INSIDIOUS FAMILY VIOLENCE IS. IT'S SOMETHING THAT CREEPS UP SLOWLY, IT DOESN'T START WITH THE PERPETRATOR PUNCHING YOU IN THE FACE.**

the three and half years we were in a relationship, followed by ten years of stalking. This perpetrator subjected me to severe verbal, emotional and physical abuse, where he isolated me from my loved ones and coercive control was a constant factor. He would call me every derogatory name and I was regularly punched, kicked, strangled and burned. One time he broke my wedding ring finger because I had asked him if he could turn the TV off, which he refused to do.

Each day became about survival, and I felt like I was living in a war zone. Home became a prison for me, trying to concentrate at uni became impossible so I dropped out, work was a form of temporary escape and relief, however it was humiliating having to make up fake excuses as to why I was yet again covered in horrible bruises or had broken bones. I will never forget the birthday where he held me hostage at gunpoint and wouldn't allow me to leave the house. When I called the police for assistance, he was successful in convincing them that nothing was going on as he put on his customary fake charm. They did not even attempt to search for the gun, something which has always completely amazed me. The police did not remove him from the house and place me in a position of safety as they should have done, instead they asked if I wanted to leave. I did. The police drove me to Southern Cross Station and dropped me off there as I had informed them that I had family in the country I could travel to be with.

The reality of what happened next was that I was too scared to get on a train back to the country, even though that is what I wanted to do more than anything in the world. I longed to be at my childhood home at the farm, cuddling my beloved dog Chep and crying to my dad who has always been my rock of strength at times of crisis. I did not do that though, instead I jumped on the first train that came for the Upfield line and went straight back to my house in Brunswick. Such was the level of power and control that John had over me that I was more scared of what he would do if I did not return. I was also worried what he might do to the house. The lease was in my name, and most of the furniture and other possessions belonged to me. I was really concerned that if I did not face the music and return to him that he would go on an orgy of destruction. I was not ready to tell my family what I was going through at this point, so I went back to my house of horrors.

I stayed with my abuser for three and a half years, however, during this time I attempted to leave him several times – as many family violence survivors do before they can safely leave. The thing which kept me with him for so long was fear. Every time I would start packing to leave, he would hold a knife to my throat and say if I left him, he would kill me and bury me in the backyard and then he would go after my friends and family members. The level of abuse and violence I experienced from this man caused me to develop depression and become suicidal, which are health issues I'd never experienced prior to that relationship.

There came a tipping point though, and this came in the form of an obnoxious, filthy, homeless man who had decided randomly to take up residence in the growing pile of rubble which was forming in the backyard of the house next door to ours which was being demolished. His name was Harry and as he cheerfully informed us, he had recently been released from Thomas Embling Hospital's high security forensic mental health unit due to committing arson. He was just the sort of lost soul that John liked to take pity on and befriend. I too, am an extremely compassionate person who likes to advocate for and assist people experiencing homelessness or suffering from a mental illness in whatever way I can, however my gut instinct was telling me, with big alarm bells and huge flashing lights, that this man was dangerous and extremely bad news. My suspicions about Dirty Harry, as I had started referring to him as in my head, were very quickly justified. He loved nothing more than jumping out to scare me in the dark when I was walking past the gate of the house he was squatting at. Dirty Harry, it turns out, was also an unlikely film buff. He particularly enjoyed regaling us with his review of how amazing he thought the ultra-violent French film *Baise-moi* was. He found the rape scene inspirational, and according to him, the woman who endured it 'completely deserved it'. So, it became a major concern to me when I discovered that John and his brothers were allowing Dirty Harry into our house to use our bathroom and wash his clothes. I communicated with John how unsafe this man made me feel. The response I received was that I was overreacting, that Dirty Harry was harmless, and I should continue to make him welcome in our home.

Around this time, posters started to go up along our street stating that a neighbour's cat Thomas was missing. I had not seen the cat and did not think much further about the 'Missing' posters until a horrific incident occurred on one sunny autumn day. John, his brothers, and I were walking back home from the shops when, like a jack-in-the-box, Dirty Harry popped out of the gate next to ours just as we went past. He invited us in for lunch. I immediately felt nauseous at the possibility of what we were about to encounter, but the look John gave me at that moment made it apparent I would not be able to excuse myself and go into our house. Dirty Harry had a pet dog, which was a skinny flea-bitten mongrel of dubious heritage that liked to snap at your ankles if you crossed its path. The dog greeted our arrival into its territory with a snarl twisting up its ugly features. To me, the pet and its owner bore a very striking resemblance. Dirty Harry camped next to the pile of building rubble in an open-sided shed with a simple rusted corrugated iron roof. He almost constantly had a campfire burning. With a great

TRAPPED.

deal of trepidation, I sat down with the lads and waited to see what lunch was. Although I am a farm girl and not scared of a bit of dirt, when I saw the meat he was offering us, the level of hygiene was definitely a concern for me. I did not really fancy a bout of food poisoning, so I politely declined what I was offered, saying I was not feeling too well. The lads did go through with eating the meat and gave appreciative thanks. At this moment, Dirty Harry decided it was the right time to declare, 'You know that meat you were just eating there, boys, do you know what that was?' The lads said they did not have a clue. 'Well, you know all those posters up for that missing cat? Well, you just ate Thomas!' With that Dirty Harry fell onto the ground in fits of laughter, whilst John and his brothers were stunned into silence with looks of shock on their faces. I took that moment to excuse myself.

It was not long after this, that emotionally I hit rock bottom. I felt so trapped in my circumstances with my relationship with John, and having the stress of this horrible, damaged man squatting next door just made things so much worse. It was early one morning, and I went into the upstairs bathroom with the intention of attempting suicide. I honestly could not face another moment living with the abuse I was enduring. It was at this moment of sheer desperation that I noticed out of the window that overlooked next door's backyard, Dirty Harry was sitting peacefully at his campfire, having a cigarette and patting his dog. The smoke from the fire curled up into the sky and danced playfully with the breeze. I stood there looking out the window for the longest time, completely transfixed by the scene playing out below me. I thought to myself, *If a man as clearly disturbed as Dirty Harry can find happiness and peace in a pile of rubble, whilst here I am feeling like a prisoner of my own mind and my own home, then something is clearly wrong.*

That moment was what finally helped me to find the resolve within myself that I had to get out of that house before either John killed me or I killed myself. I finally managed to escape this man after multiple attempts to leave him. What followed was ten years of stalking and harassment which was so terrifying, that one night I was so scared to come home because of the threats he was making, it placed me in a situation of vulnerability which resulted in me being raped by a stranger.

In 2010, I unfortunately met the man who was to become my second perpetrator of abuse. Patrick was a charming, funny Irish backpacker with model good looks, who I instantly connected with the moment we started chatting at the bar at P.J. O'Brien's. This whirlwind romance moved so quickly that he moved into my home only a week after we had met. He left six and half years later, after subjecting me to every type of abuse imaginable. The fact that he was six years younger than me and had a complex relationship with drugs and alcohol allowed me to justify many of his problematic behaviours. I kept thinking, *If only he would get help for these issues, he would not treat me like crap anymore.* However, as I now know, he did not have to be intoxicated to abuse me physically, sexually, emotionally or verbally. As the relationship progressed, he increasingly perpetrated these behaviours towards me when he was sober as well. When he walked out on me in 2016 to be with the woman, who unbeknownst to me, he had been having an affair with, he left me close to seventy thousand dollars indebt. This was a result of the financial abuse he subjected me to due to his addictive behaviours. I was then to discover that I had fallen pregnant to him. Patrick's actions towards me around the time we separated caused me to miscarry my baby daughter. Breanna was a child I had been longing to conceive for many years and it almost broke me completely when I lost her.

As a result of the abuse and trauma I have endured throughout my adult life, I now suffer from PTSD, depression and anxiety, as well as several ongoing physical injuries from the assaults I was subjected to. I have been continually failed and let down by the services and organisations meant to support and protect you when these types of crimes are perpetrated against you. I have been able to reclaim my voice and sense of identity by becoming a family violence survivor advocate. Through speaking out at events and to the media and being part of consultations around policy and legislative reforms, I have been able to become the phoenix rising from the ashes of my past.

As a tribe of supportive warrior women has grown around me who have often had shared lived experiences of abuse, I have felt safe to make submissions to various official processes such as the Victorian Royal Commission into Family Violence. It will be one of the proudest achievements of my life, that my testimony at the Royal Commission led to two of the final 227 recommendations, one of which resulted in the complete Review of the Victims of Crime Assistance Act which was tabled to the Victorian State Parliament in 2018. My advocacy work has been both lifesaving and life-changing for me, and every day the fire of passion is ignited in me to continue fighting to improve outcomes for victim survivors of family violence. Last year I was appointed to the Victims of Crime Consultative Committee by the Victorian Minister for Victim Support. I was also appointed to Victoria Legal Aid's 'Specialist Family Violence Court Project' Steering Committee. Despite everything I have survived, I feel stronger now than I ever have, and I am hopeful for the future. I may not have achieved the white picket fence dream I longed for as a child, but ultimately life has chosen a much greater purpose for me to fulfil.

Shame

SHAME.
Lala

'What! you don't you like head?' was a common question I would get when girl chats became about sex. Their mouths would droop with a look of confusion in their eyes.

'No, I don't enjoy it. I feel nothing, so there is no point,' was always my response.

'That's crazy, it's the best thing ever!' one would say, confirming with the rest of the women with a nod of agreement. I would sit there and shrug my shoulders, continuing to listen to them and their love of receiving head from their partners and how it is the best thing in the world. I believe them too, because they always make an orgasmic facial expression when saying it. Here I am – the odd one out, wishing I could get the orgasm and the feeling that they do. I felt a part of my sexuality was missing, that a part of *me* was missing. In my twenties, I would go through with the act if a partner wanted to do it, I felt numb down there like there was no feeling. All I could do was pretend to enjoy it, and that is what I did every time. Did I even care that I was faking it? No, if it made them happy, I just went along with it. I did not understand how all my girlfriends enjoyed it so much, I did not know what all the fuss was about. Eventually I just stopped doing it all together.

I came into this world as a very wanted baby. My mother and father desperately wanted a little girl, and there I arrived, making their wish granted. I was told that I was the easiest baby with soft cries and slept very well. My mother was the eldest girl of a family of eleven, and like a full leader, she took control and looked after her siblings while her parents worked. My mother was overly ambitious and ensured she got the education she needed as she saw that there was not much of a life in the Philippines, and she wanted more. My dad, he was one of six boys and one girl. My dad's parents, Mama and Papa, were overwhelmed with the children, so my dad was sent to live with his aunty, the eldest child. From my understanding, his aunty ruled the house with a strict thumb, my dad was very much abused as a child.

> **FOR ME, I FOUND THROUGH IT ALL THAT THERE WAS ALWAYS A LIGHT AT THE END OF THE TUNNEL, AND EACH BATTLE I FOUGHT AND OVERCAME, A NEW, STRONGER AND FIERCER WOMAN STOOD.**

The evening my parents met was when my mum was working as a manager at her local cinema canteen. My dad would come and see her every night, he fell deeply head over heels with my mother. My mother played hard to get, though not on purpose. She wanted to save herself for the right man. My dad fought his way to win her heart, even though if it meant breaking the hearts of many other girls along the way.

So, there I came into their world in 1985. I was their second child; my brother was four years older than me. We migrated to Perth in 1986, when I was eleven months old. My parents took up residence with family, where we stayed until I was four years old.

Eventually we moved into a house which we shared with an old man. This old man, his name was Warren. My memory of Warren was that he was very old with grey hair and bad psoriasis. But I have fond memories of him, he was kind, gentle and caring, and I always remember him sitting on an old wiry metal chair watching television. One day I never saw Warren again, he just disappeared, it was not until later I found out he had died from cancer.

My mother found a job in a factory and took on nursing studies. There she met a woman she connected with straight away, they became the best of friends, inseparable. My father worked hard and together they built their first house.

Do you know when you are small and the world seems so big? To me this house was huge – a mansion. I could see the building that was to be my new school and the footpath leading to it. It seemed like such a forever walk to get there. I loved our house and everything in it – the soft flooring, the carpet, my first and very own bedroom.

My mother eventually graduated as a registered nurse and got work straight away. She wanted the absolute best for my brother and I when it came to providing for us. There was always cooked food ready for breakfast and dinner. She wanted us to each have a waterbed, and just like that, we all had our own waterbeds. I must admit, growing up having a waterbed, I can tell you that they are not that great. I would swap a waterbed for a mattress any day.

Mum and Dad decided that they did not want us to learn their language, Tagalog, they wanted us to learn English. They only spoke to us in English. It is something they regret not teaching us.

Mum spoilt me with so much love and affection, she always did this thing that I have continued with my own children. Instead of kissing me, she would rub her nose to my cheek or ear and smell me. It may seem weird, I know. But instead of a kiss, she would take on her daughter's scent. Mum always smelt amazing, there has not been a day where she smelt awful. She always put pride in her appearance and if not for herself, she did it for her husband. My dad was very doting on my mum, they were openly affectionate in front of my brother and I. Always kissing and flirting with each other.

One of Dad's greatest all-time hobbies was fishing and crabbing. He would take us all with him or go on his own and always came back with a bucket of the night's dinner. My mother and brother were very much alike, but I took after my dad. We eventually would go fishing and crabbing just the two of us. Sometimes I would have a break from the ocean and leave Dad to it, then you could find me climbing and jumping along the big boulders and rocks and see a stray cat or two.

There was another hobby that my father had a slight obsession with – porn. As a child I would find it anywhere and everywhere. Under the bed, between the lounge cushions, behind the fridge. There were videotapes, books and comics. Sometimes I would wake up and see a glimmer of light near the hallway and I would sneak and see what was happening. It was always the small square television with people having sex in all kinds of positions in my full view and my father's back towards me.

I used to love crawling into bed with my mother, inhaling her perfume and snuggling against her warmth. One night I went to crawl into her bed, and she was not there. I heard my dad coming so I hid in the dark near a wall. My dad was carrying my mother like a bride into bed, tucking her in. He stepped back and saw me in the fetal position. *He found me,* I thought, fear ripping through me. I remember he grabbed me by my shoulders, squeezed tight and took me to my room. He then threw me like a pile of rubbish hard into bed and walked away. He stayed silent through the process.

My dad was great – loving, funny and affectionate but there was a dark side to him that came out every now and then. He always did things in silence, like pinch me hard till it bruised, always in the side of my ribs. He liked throwing me a lot, just picking me up a flinging me away. It worked, I remained silent, on my best behaviour. You may wonder if I told my mother any of this, I never did, and she never suspected.

We did not really have many toys growing up, but we cared for and loved the toys we did have so much. Mum surprised me one day with a Barbie doll. My heart leapt out of my chest with such gratefulness. It took a while before she let me take it out of the box and play with it. She wanted it to always be put back in the box. I never asked for anything, no matter how much I wanted something. I wanted a dolls' house very badly so I decided to make one out of shoe boxes, toilet rolls and anything else I could find. Tissue paper would become the dolls' blankets and cracker boxes the dolls' beds. These are my fondest memories – alone, relaxed, mystified in my own thoughts and tinkering away.

My parents were sponsoring my dad's parents – Mama and Papa – to live in Australia. They had this idea that they could live with us and help them care for my brother and I while my parents worked. This is exactly what happened.

I was six years old when Papa and Mama arrived to stay with us, moving in and getting comfortable in the spare bedroom at the other end of the house. I took to them as any grandchild would, with love and adoration. Papa and Mama had this scent to them, it was not cologne or the smell of flowers, but a mouldy clothing smell. But Papa had this distinct smell separate from Mama's that, to this day, if I come across that smell, I immediately think of him.

Mama, from memory, was a hard woman with a strict voice, she never laid a finger on me, but her voice alone was enough to set me into action. She was a loving and attentive woman but had an authoritative demeanour about her. Once I accidentally spilt milk on the table and she told me to clean it up. I do not know why I did what I did, but instead of going into the kitchen and getting a cloth, I grabbed the cushion from the lounge I was sitting on instead. Thinking she was not watching I placed the cushion on top until all the milk had dissolved and disappeared. I realised my mistake when I heard Mama fly into a vocal rage. I did not understand her as she was speaking my parents' language, but she was mad. Papa must have heard the commotion because he suddenly appeared at the doorway and immediately came to my defence. He spoke to Mama then knelt and hugged me.

My favourite chocolate back then was Picnic. I had one that I was saving and the day I decided I wanted to eat it, was the day my brother decided to eat it instead, he had his own and had already devoured it. I distinctly remember the betrayal I felt, and I started to cry. Papa came to the rescue again and said he would take me to the shop to buy more chocolate. I felt special and loved, just me, *He is taking just me to get chocolate. We are going for a walk to the deli, and he is going to spend quality time with just me.* At the deli he would tell me to get whatever I wanted, and I made sure to buy one for my brother as well. Papa held my hand as we walked the short way home. Oh boy, did I feel so special. He was my papa and I loved him very much.

One day, my parents were at work, Mama was out, and my brother was glued to the television watching *Transformers*. I was in my room and Papa came in, closing the door behind him. He tickled me slightly, and as always, I giggled. He was talking about playing with me and said I should take my clothes off. I did not want to because it was cold. Thinking nothing of it at the time I allowed him to undress me anyway. He pulled my shirt off over my head and my pants down and all that was left was my underwear. Papa pulled them down too and placed me gently on my desk. At the time I was a little confused, but not scared at all – simply confused. I had showered with Mum and Dad before, but they always prompted me to wash my body myself. This was something entirely new to me, but I went with it anyway. This was Papa and I trusted him and through the whole process he still made me laugh and giggle. Papa started to kiss my body, starting on my shoulder, he worked his way down to my chest area, sucking away at my six-year-old nipples. It tickled so much that I wiggled, he then worked his way down and opened my legs. He was down there for quite some time and every now and then he would say, 'Don't tell Mum and Dad, huh?'

I asked, 'Why?' He would say this is just for us and that my parents would not believe me. So, there it was, Papa and I had a little secret.

The next day, I went to the toilet, I was in a lot of pain and cried when I weed – it burned. It kept getting worse and I was in excruciating pain. When Mum got home from work, she saw how much pain I was in and took me to the emergency ward at the hospital. Nowadays, to check for a urinary tract infection, it's as simple as weeing in a cup, sticking a dipstick into it and checking for leukocytes and blood, then sending the sample off to the lab. I am sure there was a similar procedure back then, but because I was in the emergency ward, I was wheeled to a shared area, a male doctor came, and Mum pulled my pants down and he examined my private area, thoroughly. Oh, how I remember that moment, that feeling, how the room looked with so many bright lights. I felt awkward and just pretended I was not attached to the lower half of my body. I did have my first urinary infection. To this day, I still suffer from chronic UTIs. I found out later in life that if you experience a UTI before you are seventeen years old then you are prone to have chronic UTIs for life. Fun!

Papa would make sure that Mama was out of the house or having a nap and that my brother was at school or watching television before taking me back into my room. Always doing the same thing repeatedly. This was our daily routine for months and during those months I would get recurrent infections. 'Always wipe front to back, darling,' Mum would always say.

One day, Papa decided to change it up, and instead, once we were in my room, he laid on my bed and sat me directly on top of him. We were fully clothed, but he unzipped his pants, showed me his 'toy' and asked me to play with it. I looked at it and laughed thinking, *What on earth is that? Oh gross, it's disgusting.* He grabbed my little hands and wrapped them around his penis, the smell was awful I made an 'ewww' sound and he laughed. He fondled me while I jerked him off. 'Don't tell Mum or Dad, okay?' he said and I nodded. This continued for about eight months.

I was an artistic kid, and instead of learning in class, I would be found doodling. I did not draw stick figures but realistic people, naked and rubbing on top of each other. One day, my year one teacher, Mrs Gardener, saw them and took them from me. That evening she came to my house to have a meeting with my parents. My mum made this amazing homemade bowl of spring rolls for her, and they were talking in the living room. When she left, my parents never spoke to me about what she said but I did see my drawings in the bin. Nothing came of it.

I used to play with the boy next door who was a year older than me. One day I was in his room with him, and I got him to lay on the bed, I sat on him and we started to grind each other fully clothed. We both thought it was hilarious. He was in hysterics and so was I, we both thought it was a game. His mum came into the room and caught us. That afternoon, Mum was at work and my dad was informed of what happened and I got a good solid beating. The next day I was at the front of the house with Dad and the boy's mother next door came over to speak to Dad, asking if I had been punished. Hell, I had. I flipped the inside of my bottom lip to show her the deep cut I received from getting a good beating from Dad, pus and all.

When I was seven, Papa and Mama moved into their own home and would come visit every now and then. One night my mum and I were arguing in the hallway, I don't recall what it was about, but she was yelling at me, and I yelled back, 'Fine, I won't tell you that Papa touches me.'

My mother paused, turned around, her expression a mix of hurt, pain and shock. 'What?' she said.

'Papa touches me, Mummy,' I replied innocently. Dad was in the kitchen, and he remained like a silent puppy, frozen and listening, he did not move from his chair.

Mum proceeded to ask me several questions all at once. 'What do you mean he touches you? Like hugs you and kisses you?'

I shake my head 'no', I can see the worry in her eyes and at that moment I knew I did something wrong; I told our secret when I promised I would not. Tears were welling in my eyes.

'Where does he touch you, darling?' Mummy was calm, her voice hard but loving. I pointed to my groin area and stayed silent. The next thing, I did not expect, I thought she would be mad at me and continue to yell at me. She instead scooped me up and held me tight, I could hear her sobs. 'How long, darling? How long has this been going on for?' I heard her say.

'Since they lived with us.' Mum was so upset that I didn't tell her as soon as it happened. I could tell she was disappointed in me a little that I could not tell her.

I was in the hallway with Mum later that night and Dad was on the telephone to Papa. They were talking in their language. My dad was a soft man with a big heart, and he loved his dad very much. And he proved that love by what he was about to do next. Of all the things that were done to me and my body, my dad's words affected me the most. Papa could touch me, sexually, I didn't care, but what my dad said killed me, it will affect me for the rest of my life. Dad put his hand over the receiver, looked at me and said, 'But Papa said you let him.'

I experienced my first foster home when I was fourteen years old. I had terrible eyesight and struggled to see the whiteboard in class. I mentioned it to my dad about needing glasses. I suffered through spring with terrible allergies, one night I was rubbing my eyes because the relief felt so good. Suddenly I was knocked to the ground, Dad had hit my head. As I looked up at him, he was a horrible sight to behold, his face had contorted with anger, and he was biting his bottom lip. I knew what that meant, when Dad bit his bottom lip it meant my brother or I were going to get a belting. He grabbed me by my shoulders and threw me to the wall, he then dug his fists into my eyes, rubbing them. 'This is why you need glasses, huh, huh?' He then threw me about the hallway until finally he threw me into the lounge and walked away.

I laid in bed that night hoping, praying, that Mummy would come and sniff me goodnight once she came home from afternoon shift. I knew she would as she did it every night when she got home. I wanted Mummy; I wanted her safe arms. At 11pm I heard the garage door open, my heart fluttered, *My mummy is home,* my gentle, loving mummy. I waited for her to come to my room, heart racing. She did not. I heard my dad intercept her and lavish her with kisses. That night was different – she did not come to me or my brother, she went straight into her room. There was a big painful lump in my throat, and I cried and screamed into my pillow until sleep took me. The next day I was a wreck at school and all I had to do was tell one student and then the next minute I was in the principal's office with two social workers.

What happened to me affected me for years to come. How I thought relationships were supposed to be. When I turned fifteen, I was not into boys as much. Just crushes here and there.

One day my father left suddenly, he ran away with my mother's best friend. Abandoned us. With Dad not around and Mum working double shifts to take her mind off her depression, I started to look for father figures on the internet. I did not know at the time, it was only when I received counselling that it made sense – I would talk to men in their thirties on the internet, striking up a relationship. One man I spoke to was thirty-one and he had a webcam, he told me that we should cybersex. Sixteen-year-old me watched him jerk off on camera while he read my messages.

I could have turned to recreational addiction to help me cope with what I have been through. And honestly, reading back over this, I am thinking, *Is my story even worthy to be told when countless others have experienced far worse than I have?* Maybe not.

But in the end, I am worthy. It took years to believe it, but I finally got there.

I am strong, through the chaos of it all I kept walking.

And I am loved, and the main love came from within.

Today I stand, proud of the woman I am and what I have overcome, what I have achieved and my mentality. I am a huge advocate for people to understand the importance of their sexuality. To know what sexual abuse is, what defines it. What is not acceptable. To not be afraid to speak up, to scream and yell if they must ... to be heard. You are not alone, and you will get through it.

For me, I found through it all that there was always a light at

the end of the tunnel, and each battle I fought and overcame, a new, stronger and fiercer woman stood.
    LALA

Alone

ALONE.

Bronwyn

Let me share a story with you, perhaps you will choose to believe it, perhaps not. I have spoken of this story before, nothing changes, because it is one where I only remember details, feelings, terror and pain. My story has many chapters, but for now, I will give you one.

Putting words on paper seems difficult, the retelling of something I so desperately wanted to escape is painful to relive. I've spoken the words so many times; I know the looks people give me – the glazed look in their eyes, the disbelief on their faces and then the silence. That silence. It only lasts for a few seconds, but you can see the thought processes and comprehension of a story that can only be fictitious. After all, I don't look like I am a victim. I have nice clothes, I present well, I stand tall, I am educated and I can communicate efficiently. How can I be a victim of domestic violence? How can I spin a tale that is best suited for a storybook? The only answer bundled in the minds of people is that I am lying, my story is set for the big screen. A performance meticulously orchestrated. I know that look, I know it very well. The thing that really bothers me, not so much the disbelief – because let's be honest, we all want to live in a world of peace and happiness – not the terror where I spent thirteen long years hiding at every opportunity. But the one thing that really frustrates me about my story is that when my words are seen, they are experienced firsthand by those I have spoken to – but they have lived a very small portion of what I have lived, and it is almost like a sigh. An exhale of burdened air, their eyes open up and you can almost see a light shining above their head as my words finally show a truth, a reality of facts understated and shied with modesty. It is at that point that I always turn around and walk away, because why could you not believe me, why could you not hear me, my pain and my torture? It always puzzles me as to why my words could not ring true to you and you had to first experience what I lived?

It has been a process, as the date stands, over six years. I have healed, I am still healing. For so long, I travelled a dark tunnel that just never had light. It felt as though I would never see a glimmer of light that gave hope, that maybe, just maybe, even after the torturous thirteen years, my journey would end. Maybe, just maybe, I will be normal? I often follow the saying 'what is normal for the spider is chaos for the fly'. Such true words, and yet, when the web of information is given, we are still told to be like the fly. Maybe the idea of flying is supposed to make us free? Well, my web started a long time ago.

I'll take you back to a moment when I learnt of a new fear. A new terror. I mean, don't get me wrong, when you have objects or words flying at you, or you feel your own power as a women be taken from you in violating sexual acts where saying no meant nothing – you do break, you tend to learn to block out life. You escape in your own mind, where if he cannot get to you, in that safe little box in your head, it doesn't matter what he does to your body, you will be okay, just stay in the box. That fear, I knew how to hide from, I had a safe place to go. The new fear, the one where you don't know, you don't know how, where or when he is coming at you. Now that fear was new to me and even though

I could stand in corridors filled with security watching diligently, people cowering in corners or slipping into rooms that would decide their fate within the judicial system, I learnt a fear that couldn't protect me. Dressed elegantly, standing tall, I would still shake. I would tremble in fear and even the reassuring hands guiding me, I no longer knew the demon hunting me. *Follow the rules, do as they say, speak the truth.* Words I'd mutter to myself, as I placed every hope and faith I had in a system that would grant me freedom from a hell that I lived in.

It is said that once you leave a violent relationship, that this is when the victim gets hurt the most. The perpetrator loses control and hence will do anything to get that control back. I didn't know this, if I had, perhaps my decisions would have been a little different. Perhaps the last words that he spat out me wouldn't have been, 'The only way that you are getting out of this relationship is in a box.' Perhaps if he hadn't hissed those words to me, that Sunday night in June on my daughter's birthday, at my bedroom door when I mustered up the courage to say I want a divorce as he stormed out of the house on another 'boys night', I would have only left in a box?

Perhaps, if my father had not knocked on my door at 1am on that Monday morning, having driven to my house in his pyjamas for no reason, no phone call, no message, just a quiet angel reaching out for me to come and help, that I would have never had the strength to say, 'Grampa, I'm coming home. Tomorrow we are coming home.' Perhaps, if none of that had unfolded, I would not be standing petrified and ready to fight with every bit of my body and soul for me and my children. Perhaps there would have been a quiet funeral? All I know, that as I stepped into the scraps of sunlight that crept through the windows to get warm, I was going to keep going until the day I knew that I was safe and that my babies were happy. I would straighten my shoulders, sit up a little more, hold my head high and do my best to hide my fear as I stood there in the hallways of justice.

'You have nothing to fear, it is all in your head.' It is strange that when you are asked about events that happened, the response is always the same. You made it up. It is in your head. It most certainly didn't feel like a fictitious story when I felt his wrath. It was easier to deal with his tempers when I was asleep. Usually after a 'boys' night or day out' he would come home – that's a funny word, home, most certainly wasn't a place that was safe. But he would come back and we would hide. I would go to my room, my closet. How comfortable it became to hide in the far back corner where you could see the shadows move, at least the devil himself knew I was there. I could seek shelter with the shadows and I would be safe. When I wasn't hiding he would find me, even if it meant I was asleep. Bundled in my bed, warm under the covers, he would come into the bedroom. Thinking back, my room was not a safe place to be. Every encounter brought new terror, but those shadows in the far corner where he couldn't find me – now, that was a safe place. He would throw his huge frame into the room in the middle of the night after these days or nights outs with the boys, flinging his arms frantically, punching the air with hysteria. The light would get smacked on and he would stoop his large six-foot-plus body over me and fling the blankets back off of me in one swift violent motion. The blankets would fly across the room and as they crashed to the floor, so did his temper. It's almost as though you're in a movie, where what you see doesn't seem real, where you want to tell the main character what to do but you can't because this is real, and the shock of surprise gets you off guard every time. He would fly into a rage, spitting whilst he violently blurted out words and accusations that made no sense.

He would throw his body around the room and hover over me to remind me that I was smaller than him and that he had the right to do whatever he pleased. I still don't understand those nights, those moments. I would simply escape to that safe box that I had become safe in, the shadows that had become my home and safe haven. And as quickly as he blasted his way into the room, he would leave. I never followed, that would be a bad choice and as I get told 'it's all in your head' by people meant to protect me, they were never there. At least I knew how to deal with the demon that spat profanities and vile words and made me believe that I was nothing more than scum on the bottom his shoe, but now, as I confide my story, my life, my experience, I don't know what his rage will do. I only know that if and when he comes near me, I do not want to be on my own.

The endless list of questions I was asked in the carpeted silent halls, why didn't you leave before, why did you get married, why didn't you ask for help, why did you not protect your children? It is almost as if these questions will suddenly unravel my life as my bad decision, my own bad choice. A justification as to why someone would treat another with such hostility and violence and hatred. I married the monster who tortured me every day because I thought it would make things better. That maybe if he looked at me as I walked down the aisle, radiant and beautiful, a princess, he would see that I was everything he ever wanted. He would change and I would get to live that happily-ever-after story forever. Getting to that aisle was a battlefield, and oh, how I was wrong. So very wrong. My wedding was made special by my parents, the two people who actually witnessed the true monster that he was on numerous occasions. My mum got dressed with me that morning, helped me dress my little girl and do her hair. My mum did her absolute best to make my magical day so very special. I had no friends, after years of not being allowed out, or my friends were made to feel very uncomfortable around him – I was isolated. I was hoping that this day would change everything.

I wore a gorgeous off-white lace dress. The fabric cascaded down my body in a small train. The detail of lace and beads sat perfectly on my bosom. I picked out shoes that matched my dress, and my hair was softly tied back in flowing curls. I wanted to be the princess. The fairytale of every little girl's dream. It was a nightmare that I was only meant to live, and that I did on that day. As I walked down the aisle, he was annoyed at me because the sun was too bright at the beach. As we had the photos taken, he was in his element of having attention but I was in the way. At the reception, he complained about the food, the venue, the company and this was all my fault. My smiles came from my beautiful two little children; they kept my heart smiling that day.

It is funny what people do and don't see. Whilst there were people, I only had to wear the verbal punishment. But that night was a very different story. I don't know where he went; I only know that when he came back he was angry that I wouldn't have sex with him, angry that I wouldn't get up after falling asleep to have a spa bath with him. I felt his temper that night as he spat words of pure hatred towards me. I was reminded yet again of how useless, pathetic and empty I was. I was also told that I looked horrible and that I would never be a beautiful bride. I was also told that it was his right to have me as his wife sexually. That day, sadly, was one of the worst days of my life. As I shared this story with systems designed to help people, I was told that without medical evidence, there is very little help and that there would be a lot of his-word-against-mine.

As for leaving, I did that too. How many times I had been told of stories of women leaving and then going back. Stupid move, you would think, why didn't you learn the first time? It's a hope, it's the story we are fed as children. Maiden gets saved by handsome prince and they live happily ever after. Building a life with a partner and building that perfect home with the white picket fence.

> **"HEY, LITTLE FIGHTER, SOON THINGS WILL GET BRIGHTER.**

The happily ever after. Maybe, just maybe, because he knows that I don't want to be mistreated, he will change? The famous words, *he will change*.

Yes, I left. My fourth child was a baby, it was April, and I remember the moment so well. His mother had come to Australia for a visit over Easter; she stayed in our family home. Now don't get me wrong, having family is a great thing, but to be told by her that I am an awful mother – days after I had given birth to my fourth child – or that I am not housewife material and I should run after her son more, doesn't give you much faith in their belief systems. The air could be sliced with a hot butter knife, it was icy cold, but not from the weather. It was the hostility that ran rife in that house, the snarky comments and the foul looks of disapproval. You could not tread any more lightly than we did.

That fateful day, I suggested he take his mother out, and that he should spend more time with her. We were in a back room. I knew that his mother felt bored being at the house and I felt for her because that was my life – four walls and a window. A prison without bars. I don't know why I felt the need to speak up for the woman that belittled me at every opportunity, but I did. And I asked him. It was as if something snapped in him. How dare I speak up?

He flew into an uncontrollable rage, his arms went everywhere, his fists punched anything that was in the way, and he pushed his body into mine and screamed in my face. I could feel every bit of spit land on my face. His anger was intense, it was explosive. And then he grabbed me, his hands grasped my shoulders and started shaking me violently. His strength lifted me onto my toes and I could feel my body being forced into the air. As many times as I felt his temper, this was the first time I actually thought that he was going to kill me. And then he pushed me back with such force that I struggled to gain my footing and fell. I jumped up and ran, I grabbed my phone called my parents, grabbed my children and hid us away until my parents came to our rescue. And all this time, his mother just stood there, not saying a word, almost as if she approved of his actions. What followed were days of him begging me to come back, he would change; we would get counselling, we would be better. His crocodile tears were convincing, I believed it, at least I wanted to believe what he said. And I went back. Life never got back to a blissful normal, I trod more carefully, I kept my voice quiet and I kept my children quiet.

It's been a few years now, my journey through stairways, corridors, offices and courtrooms have finally left me feeling a sense of stillness, of peace. I have learnt to embrace my own journey and I am grateful, as I step out of the last building that would decide my fate, that I am in control of my own life. I no longer shake uncontrollably; I no longer shiver in fear. I can stand tall and hold my head up bravely and with immense courage, because I fought a battle for thirteen years to stay alive and then I fought a new unknown battle for my freedom and the happiness of my family. I will always know that there are some things in life that will trigger me, but that control lies in my ability to know that I alone can influence how I feel and how I want my life to go. Knowing that, I have let go and set myself free from the cage he placed me in. I will not give him a name; I will not give him immortality. I will let him become faceless, unknown and dead to me. For so long I hoped that someone would shine a light for me, to show me the way, to give me a helping hand. I crawled my way through that darkness, I danced with shadows that no-one should ever see, and I lived in a hell of biblical proportions. Maybe now my story will end with my own version of my happily ever after, a story from terror to freedom. One thing that I do know is that I am not the fly. I am the spider and I will embrace every web that I weave to live happily ever after.

emotional

EMOTIONAL.
Shel

There are so many memories that came to mind when I started writing my chapter – abuse from my dad, abuse from my mum, abuse from a teacher who smacked me once in class in primary school, abuse from a manager once throwing a stapler at one of my colleagues or that companies push onto their staff with inflexible working hours or high KPI demands, emotional abuse from romantic relationships and fights with friendships throughout the years. All to varying degrees, but all have impacted me in different ways.

I have realised, though, through writing this, that there is little education and understanding about the impacts we play in each others' lives and until there is, the cycle continues.

I don't believe I had a bad childhood or upbringing, I am happy with the woman I have become and believe I've needed all these experiences to help impact others. While I don't have many memories, I have glimpses of fun things, though none of them included my dad – my earliest and most favourite memories involved my mum. I remember being in Oman with my mum, grandpa and grandma. I remember spending time with my aunty, uncle, cousins and mum in Dubai. I remember a couple of family parties, I remember Mum's smile. I remember feeling shy when she was telling my brother and me about the 'birds and the bees' and I remember when we were a little older she saved and sent us on an unaccompanied minor trip to India to spend time with our family and then met us in Singapore.

Memories of my dad are the opposite. I remember a specific night I could hear him belting my mum, I could hear her screaming and crying and he made us kiss her 'better' after. I remember the day we ran away, Mum told us we were going swimming and he was sitting in one of the rooms saying goodbye as we walked out of the back door to the garage. He asked me to stay with him, he asked me not to go swimming with her. I knew something was wrong, I felt scared and sad for him. I remember the day we went back to the house with our family friends, I think that was the day they must have officially separated. Those are my childhood memories of him.

The only good one I have as a family unit was one Christmas, where he put glow-in-the-dark stickers on the ceiling and said it was Santa Claus. I knew it wasn't. That was it, all the memories I have until I was in high school.

I later found out that my mind may not remember it all, but my body hasn't forgotten a moment.

When going on this writing journey, it was meant to be with my mum ... until she started asking questions about my experiences. When I told her it was about the abuse I experienced with her and Dad, she was shocked. I was shocked that she was shocked, and it forced me to see it from another perspective yet again.

My mum wasn't perfect, none of us are. My fondest memories include her and I think the world of her now. She sacrificed so much to provide us with safety when we lived eight years without it. How could I possibly talk about the abuse I received from her?

My mum suffered through eight years of an abusive relationship. Unlike me, she would remember it all like it was yesterday,

I'm sure. I can't imagine what it would have been like having three children and being terrified each time the car pulled into the driveway, walking on eggshells every day, how scared I would feel to make a mistake knowing that my head could get shoved against the wall at any minute.

I couldn't imagine what it would have been like to be sent to boarding school, away from my family. Maybe subconsciously why mum always sent us to schools close to home?

I couldn't imagine what it would have been like running away from your husband with three plastic bags of towels and bathers with the intention of never going back home. Immigrant, three children, no assets as the home was in his name, no money, no job. I couldn't imagine being in this situation with no family support, being shunned because 'Indian girls do not leave their husbands' and receiving letters in the mail to 'stop being stubborn and spoilt and go back'. I also couldn't imagine the guilt of breaking up the much respected 'family unit' and the beautiful life that was planned on being built in such a country with the love of your life.

I am privileged to not be able to fully imagine those feelings, yet this same privilege gave me the naivety to tell my mum that she too abused me and I was going to write about it.

I wanted to write about how she kicked me out of home, how she beat me when I made a mistake, how she ignored me when she was angry, how she raked everything from my bedroom to the front garden once when I didn't clean it. The truth was, I received the brunt of Mum's aggression because I was the loudest one, the one that tested the boundaries, the one with cheek and sass.

But as I write away, thinking of all the things that weren't perfect about my upbringing, I'm well aware it isn't isolated to my family – many south-east Asian families go through the same – domestic violence, patriarchal family unit with little to no affection from parents – more than a generational issue, it's a cultural one.

From the experiences of my childhood, I was also far from perfect. I remember throwing a chair at my brother once. What child throws a chair at their big brother with so much anger? I did. I remember him crying and feeling a surge of heat throughout my entire body, feeling sick after I did it but not apologising. I was an awful sister, an awful daughter, but I didn't know how else to express myself so I acted out. It still makes me sick to my stomach when I think about how I treated my family at times and I'm not too proud to say that I still fall back into these habits to this day.

We didn't grow up in a family of saying 'I love you', we didn't hug or go around the table and say things we are grateful for like we see in the movies and like we do every Christmas now.

It's been a journey. A tremendously devastating but fulfilling one.

Dad moved back to India around 2006 and we never heard from him again. When I was travelling around India, I asked relatives for his number to call him, thought it would be nice for me to pop in, see how he was while I was visiting other family. After eight years of him being in another country with no contact, do you want to know what his response was when I asked him how he was? 'You haven't bothered to ask after all these years, why do you care now?' I remained composed the rest of the short conversation but hung up the phone and burst into tears. My partner at the time told me I shouldn't see him, but it was important for me to do the right thing so my future self didn't regret it. It was awkward as hell when I saw him but I left feeling deep compassion for the life he was now living, or … the lack of one.

To this day, none of us know why Dad turned the way he did, was it migrating to a new country? Were there mental health issues that we weren't aware of? Was it generational, was he treated that way as a child? Was it the pressure of being the provider in the family? Australia would have been (more) racist in those days. He used to work for Air India and I remember he had a job pushing a button at a sewing machine company here, earning peanuts, I remember him saying. So why did he give up so easily while Mum worked so hard in so many different fields to keep a roof over our heads and food in the fridge? How in the hell did she raise three children and pay a mortgage on even less peanuts than he was on? Questions that we will never have answers to.

Violence. Surrounded by it. I heard it from my dad, I felt it from my mum and I saw it in high school, around my peers most days. On my first day of high school, there was a fight on the oval and the teacher got kicked in the head. There were times I hung around the wrong crowd – I smoked, I drank. I had very little self-worth and no idea what a healthy relationship with anyone looked like. I was the friend that got black-out drunk most weekends that everyone had to look after. I would argue with friends and put myself in terribly dangerous situations without caring what happened to me. The weekends were the only thing I would look forward to because, whilst I felt awful after, being in it gave me a false sense of control and security. I was far from it though, relatable to many troubled teenagers I'm sure.

Somehow I didn't find violence in relationships, though I think this was attributed to seeing how fiercely independent and strong my mum became, and while I would never have told her due to our ever-changing complex and irrational relationship, I wanted to be like her. As I grew older, I was in awe of her. She went from being an English teacher in India, to a full-time wife and mother, to a single mother who was also a: travel agent, lead lighter, vending machine owner and restaurant owner. She also dragged us to

EMOTIONAL.

Amway network marketing events and she now lives a busy and quiet life with her now husband in regional Western Australia. I complained about her through it all but the woman was and is bloody brilliant, she did it all while raising three kids without any family support and very few friends. She taught me to hustle and strive without saying a word. This constant masculine energy comes with its own whirlwind of issues … so by my early twenties enter: 'I'm a strong independent woman that don't need no man and I can do anything myself so leave me alone' … which we now know, also doesn't work for a healthy relationship.

By this stage I had an idea of the person I wanted to be but my problem was that I still didn't know what a healthy relationship looked like – I would always be triggered, if anyone even slightly raised their voice I would have heat surge throughout my entire body. My amygdala was in overdrive, almost instantly I could not control what I was saying and I would see red, see fire, see hate, and go into survival mode. Flight, fight, freeze, fawn. I sure as hell picked fight each and every time, I've been choosing that since I was a kid – fight. I didn't know how to regulate my emotions and I didn't have the emotional intelligence to know there was something wrong. I was able to disconnect almost instantly from relationships and I was stubborn in a toxic way. If I wasn't in a relationship, it was a game. I didn't care if I hurt a guy. I did not think highly of men, I connected men with pain and there was no way I was going to be dependent on one, ever. I felt like being in a relationship was a waste of time because they all end anyway.

My beliefs were: men leave and relationships cause pain … and you couldn't change my mind. It was a vicious cycle … until a bearded Aussie man strolled into my life, chest out with a big grin.

This guy is no angel, but when I went through my repetitive toxic patterns and self-destructive behaviours, he was the one that reminded me each time that if I don't work on things now, then it would happen in the next relationship. If there is one thing he has, it's complete patience. I don't know why the panic attacks came back but when he would raise his (very deep) voice, I would feel heat pulse throughout my entire body, my amygdala would take over, we would fight and I would say awful things and then have another panic attack. They got so bad that he once had to carry me into the shower when I was unable to move. It wasn't normal, it wasn't sustainable, so I saw a psychologist. It was the best thing I have ever done in my entire life – and I've done a lot of great things.

My psychologist explained to me why I was the way that I was. She explained family dynamics to me and the impacts of hearing/seeing domestic violence is the reason for big emotions and the inability to regulate them. She said a father's role is to give us an understanding of how men should treat us and a mother's role is to provide support, and not having both of those growing up has had its own impacts. The psychologist gave me tools to understand myself and better navigate my emotions and reduce negative patterns, and I am pleased to say I don't have surges of heat when I'm upset and have not had a panic attack since.

It's common to hear 'it's not that bad' compared to others, I've said it myself multiple times while writing this, especially after a friend confided in me about their sexual abuse as a child, but I've realised that we can't negate our own experiences because it all matters.

I've had multiple conversations and seen abuse with people in my network that have stayed in abusive relationships to keep 'the family unit' because 'better the devil you know'. I hope this gives insight that it's impacting our children more than we realise.

My aim isn't to bring shame to my family or point fingers or create blame – my aim is to bring awareness from what I have experienced. I originally wrote about my experience in my first fictional novel and very subtly talked about it in my chapter in *The FIFO Wives' Tales,* but subtle doesn't create change. Talking about it does.

There is so much hidden and unprocessed trauma because it feels safer when no-one knows, when there's no judgement … but how will that provide a safer generation after us? How can we stop toxic behaviour? Because whether we realise it or not, it creates a subtle domino effect that impacts everyone we love whether we realise it or not – it impacts our families, romantic relationships, friendships, even how we communicate with colleagues and strangers.

I hope we can all remain kind to ourselves as we navigate our way through it – reminding each other that none of us received a guidebook to being the perfect sister, brother, mother, father, wife, husband or … human … and I quite honestly believe we really are all just doing the best we can in our unique situations.

Let's continue to spark conversation, remove guilt and shame, to create change for our generations to come.

> **YOUR EXPERIENCE IS VALID, AND IT'S IMPORTANT TO SEEK PROFESSIONAL HELP TO TALK ABOUT IT. THIS ALLOWS US TO PROCESS OUR PAST AND MOVE FORWARD WITH TOOLS TO NOT REPEAT (OR AT LEAST BE AWARE OF) UNHEALTHY BEHAVIOURS. YOU GOT THIS!**

Underestimated

UNDERESTIMATED.
Nicole

Where are my rights?

This is how my story began, I write about it now like it's not a part of me. Somehow like trying to recall a vivid nightmare or a terrible story told by a loved one.

It doesn't feel like it's my own, there is a lot of shame and guilt I still feel but somehow I'm no longer in it. It's no longer my reality.

I can only relate this to the ten years of absolute hell that I experienced being married to a complete and utter abusive sociopath.

See – things trigger me now, someone can raise their voice or they can say something which is otherwise completely innocent, and in my mind, it is turned into an absolute anxious mess that I have to try to fix and keep the peace. Adjust my behaviour to stop the next stage from happening to me.

My name is Nicole Gilbert and this is my story, I'm a mother of four beautiful boys and I now run a successful international cosmetic company.

It wasn't always this way though. My life growing up was great. I always tell people, 'I grew up in a small gold mining town in Western Australia, yeah my dad was strict and Mum and him fought a lot. But we had it really good.'

See, when you're a child you don't really know that your 'normal' is different from everyone else's normal.

On weekends we would go to my nana and grandad's house, I was extremely close to my nana. She was like a second mother to me. My mother had battles with depression and dealing with life, so she often wasn't present in the way I required emotionally as a child to grow and feel a sense of nurture.

Nana, however, taught me how to cook, how to buy fish from the fishmonger and then bring it home and make the best fish and chips ever on the wooden stove we lit with kerosene and matches.

I remember running into Nana's house one day, I went around the back as I knew she would be in the laundry outhouse washing clothes, I could already smell the washing powder she had been using.

I ran around and stopped suddenly, Nana was trying to pull herself up and was bleeding, her face was covered in blood.

I panicked and ran inside to the loungeroom and yelled, 'Dad, Grandad! Nana needs help, she has fallen and is bleeding.'

What I saw next confused me, I saw my dad get angry with grandad and my grandad muttered under his breath. Then my dad told me, 'It's okay, love, Nana will be okay.'

I couldn't understand why both of them weren't rushing to go check on her and take her to the doctor.

I felt angry at them both, I felt like I had to protect my nana even at the age of nine.

It was only later on in life, as I grew older, that I found out the true story, that Nana was being abused and had been for most of her life. But this was 'the norm', especially in old country towns.

It really was just something that was done, so by default my child-brain formed a warped sense of how others should treat us, how our emotions should be pushed aside and how we should just keep things hush-hush just to keep the peace and appear as a good solid family unit, and just be a good wife.

Fast forward to when I was sixteen years old, my parents divorced for the second time, I was told I had to find my own place to live and basically fend for myself.

I went into overdrive, I mean, going from a strict household to complete freedom – oh, and I forgot to say, undiagnosed ADHD. I was a sixteen-year-old girl who was angry at most of the men in her life, because she couldn't yet understand the complexities of the adult world.

Boy, did I go off the rails!

I was studying beauty therapy at the time, I always wanted to be a part of the beauty world, I loved it. In fact, I did so well at college that the owners asked me to work there and wanted to help me pay off the rest of my studies towards my diploma.

But it didn't matter what I did in regards to achievements, my parents seemed too preoccupied in their divorce and court battles to care about what I was doing.

I felt so misunderstood and lonely that I started seeking out that gratification in other places.

I started clubbing six to seven days a week, drinking every night. I felt amazing, free and totally in control of my life and joy.

But it soon spiralled, I met a bouncer, Eric, when I was seventeen years old. I mean, who can say, that in a world as a young girl when everyone has left you and you feel scared and alone, that a big tough bouncer wouldn't make you feel somewhat more secure?

Eric lied to me from the get-go –I was young and naive and just wanted to live in the moment – he told me he was twenty-one years old and I believed him. I later found out that he was, in fact, seven years older than me and had a kid that lived in Indonesia, his motherland, and that what I thought I knew was just all made up. By that point, I felt like I was too far in, I was homeless and living out of my car, half staying with him and his family and he swore to me no more lies and that he would tell me the truth from now on.

So I gave Eric another chance, he took that opportunity to open up and tell me everything. He said he missed his son back home so bad, Eric was crying and telling me he wanted a baby to help make him feel better. He asked if that was something I would want, he said he loved me and wanted to be with me forever.

I was eighteen then, and although I didn't love him, I was caught up in the feeling of being needed and serving a purpose.

Eric was a Muslim, and for me to continue to be with him required me to convert to Islam and follow his traditions. Now, I was raised as an atheist, I mean my proper no-religion, no-church dad said, 'Once we are dead, we are worm food,' so I had no idea what this would entail, I just thought, *Cool, I can utter some words and then it's done. That's easy.*

So I converted, I fell pregnant. Two weeks after I found out I was pregnant, Eric told me that his student visa had run out and he was being deported back to Jakarta, Indonesia.

WHAT THE FUCK!

So here I am, eighteen years old, pregnant and faced with Eric leaving and not knowing when he will return, when he says, 'Why don't you come with me?'

I said, 'My parents don't even know I'm pregnant yet! They are going to kill me!'

Surprisingly, when I called my dad, who I thought would be the worst, he said to me, 'Love, I will always support you, I'm here for you and I love you.'

My mum, however, said, 'You stupid bitch, you need an abortion, now!' This, coming from my mum, who threw a pack of condoms on my bed at sixteen when I returned from a trip back to Kalgoorlie and said, 'Since you're hanging around your old friends in Kalgoorlie, you will need those,' not knowing that I had been raped by a guy at a house party I snuck out to. I had never been with a man before, I was a virgin. I got myself into a situation where I felt like I couldn't call my mum for help. So how the hell could I tell her that after returning, so I just kept it to myself. I just thought, *If only you knew how I was really feeling.*

So with that, I felt like I had nothing keeping me in Australia so off I flew with Eric to Jakarta, and it was my home for the next five months.

I returned to Australia when I was five months pregnant and Eric still could not enter back into Australia.

I ended up giving birth to a beautiful baby boy on 20 June 2006, without Eric. I was nineteen years old, I was so frightened but I no longer felt alone.

Eric ended up returning two weeks after my son was born, as a surprise. I didn't know he was returning. He just showed up, I was getting out of the shower, I opened the shower door and *bam!* there he was. 'Surprise!' he shouts. I slammed the door in his face and screamed.

Again, I felt angry, I just hated him for using me. Because now he had a baby with an Australian woman he could gain citizenship. I was a tool, used.

It didn't work out between Eric and I.

I ended things, told him to leave when my son was eighteen months old. He was coming home drunk all the time and not being responsible at all.

I craved a solid man who knew how to be in control of his life, I wanted stability for myself and my son. Not a drunk that came home and passed out on the floor night after night.

I lived on my own for a bit and with my best friend Jody. Jody and I grew up together in Kalgoorlie. I used to run down to her house as a little girl and we would play all day. We went to kindy together and we both had troubled home life so we would bond, talk and laugh for hours on end.

Jody was living with me and my brother at that point, I was a single mum and struggling. Not only financially but emotionally. I was the oldest sibling and the only girl so I felt like I was responsible for so much. My brother, who is three and a half years younger than me, came to live with me after going through his own turmoil. My mother refused to have him and my dad, so he got a job near me and I would wake up at five each morning to take him to work and then pick him up again at home time. He had lost his licence so I had to act as fill-in mum.

I was twenty-three years old and just felt so responsible – for my brothers and my son and myself. I blamed myself for my parents' marriage breakdown, for my brother's troubles and everything else I had been through.

I just thought to myself, *If I could just have some proper solid guidance I would stop messing up.*

I reached a point where I said to Jody, 'I feel like I'm going to waste, I want more stability.' To me, that was through marriage, I wanted it immediately and in my mind with my terrible problem-solving skills (thanks, ADHD) I thought of a solution.

I mean, I was still considered a Muslim at the time, so I knew in the religion that there was not supposed to be any dating, that a man of Islamic faith who was practicing, was supposed to treat his wife with the utmost respect and care. I mean I had watched allll the youtube videos on it, what could go wrong?!

So I went ahead and arranged my own marriage … yep, I know. Hindsight is great, isn't it? I went ahead and set up to marry a man I had only been speaking to for three months. He was in Sydney,

I was in Perth. He seemed amazing, knew the religion, loved kids and love-bombed the absolute crap out of me!

I never met him physically before, the day I did was the day I arrived in Sydney and married him …

It wasn't love at first sight, or love at all. It was structure, security and stability.

I thought, *Well if others can do this, so can I.* My family had already cut me off when I converted and then had a baby and ran off to Jakarta. I mean I had nothing else to lose, in my eyes they didn't care about me, and I was trying my best to start a new life and they would never understand.

So I moved to Sydney, things were great (well, I told myself they were, always the optimist I am).

My new husband had rented out the smallest, dodgiest flat in Auburn, Sydney, I had ever seen. It was filled with mould, cockroaches and had no aircon or laundry.

But I thought, *That's okay, I can add my spin on this, I was living out of my car only a few years ago. It's an upgrade, Nicole.*

But almost immediately the red flags were there, but in subtle ways. When you search, *Am I being abused?* it comes up with what I would say are the late stages of abuse – hitting, yelling and quite obviously nasty behaviour.

See, what happens first is the grooming – I would cook a meal and he would get home and give me so much praise over something I made, even if it was instant noodles.

I can only liken it, now in hindsight, to a reward system, like you would when training a dog. You give them a treat and the dog learns to sit, after a while the treat is taken away but the dog still sits when told.

So I would go about my day-to-day activities and slowly that praise started to disappear, so I would do more. I would cook better meals, clean the house more, dress up more, do my hair, my make-up – anything to feel like I was a good person, a good wife. Like my home was stable and structured.

My husband slowly started to tell me that what I was wearing was not good and pointed at Muslim women on the streets of Sydney wearing long black abayas that they looked beautiful and how beautiful I would look if I wore one too. He put cash in my hand and said, 'Go buy the most expensive one, you deserve it.'

I didn't want to wear it, but I had never been told I deserved something before. So I felt confused but also special.

The same behaviour followed with the way I spoke and laughed, I was told that I should be quieter. That I laughed too loud, I spoke too much. That women of values are humble and only speak when they have something intelligent to say. That is where a woman holds her power, in her control of herself.

I mean this guy had it all figured out! At that time I thought *life,* but really he had *me* figured out. He knew how I worked, I loved to feel like I mattered, that I was of value and what I had to say was important.

So he spoke to me in a way which I thought I was being empowered, that I could finally stand up to my parents and people who had disowned me. I mean, my husband was always the one to remind me. He would say things like, 'I can't believe your parents would do that to you, you are amazing. They mean nothing now, I'm your world now. Don't worry about them.'

See, one of the signs of domestic abuse is alienation from loved ones, but an abuser is clever in the way they manipulate. He made every decision, but because I was the one actioning them, I felt like I was the one making them.

This is the subtlety of abuse and how it's so deeply entwined into your brain that you feel constantly agitated, you look at yourself in the mirror and no longer know who you are anymore. You don't laugh anymore, you no longer see the joy in things. You become like a peacekeeping machine, who only breathes, eats and sometimes sleeps. You plan everything around your partner and how they will react, the only thing you can feel is deep sadness and anger.

Fast forward some years later – we have three boys together and I'm a full-time stay-at-home mum, I'm involved in the community fully, my (now ex-) husband is a chef and had a cafe he would make food and I would take photos and post about it on social media. The higher I put him up on the pedestal about 'how great he was' the better I was treated at home.

I had formed friendships with some beautiful women over the ten years of being involved in that community, but I felt trapped.

I was expected to cover my hair, eat a strict halal diet, no alcohol and no music.

Heck, he even made me step into the bathroom with a particular foot, I had to say prayers before eating and after, then he would call me constantly from work and I had to pick up otherwise I would be yelled at, then ignored.

The thing that got me was this man is not a religious person at all!

I mean to the outside world he had the perfect outer shell, the perfect family and his own cafe, etc. …

But behind closed doors, this is a person who would come home with a bottle of vodka and make me drink. I had been sober for eight years and he said I wasn't fun anymore so he wanted to see me drunk. I said, 'But we are Muslim?'

He replied, 'Ahhh, no-one will know, don't worry.'

So that was it, he broke my sobriety.

He then started this every night when he would get home from work. 'I want my rights as a husband.' Sex is what he wanted. If I didn't conform he would then tell me, well, it's expected because I drink now and I'm not a good wife or person.

I believed it, I believed yet again, that my actions were because I was a bad person, that if I just did more things to make him happy then I would be a good person, and when I overexerted myself I was given praise just like I mentioned previously about the analogy of training a dog.

I was so frightened to say or do anything wrong that I was fully under his control and had no mind of my own.

He became increasing perverted sexually, he would constantly watch porn, even while we were having sex, and he would shove very large sex toys into my body and film it. If I had any objections I would get yelled and screamed at.

> **IT WAS LIKE SOMETHING SNAPPED INSIDE OF ME, SUDDENLY FLASHES OF EVERYTHING I HAD SACRIFICED AND GONE THROUGH TO APPEASE HIM WERE AT THE FOREFRONT OF MY MIND. HE UNDERESTIMATED ME ...**

I remember getting up after and washing the blood away in the shower and thinking, *Thank God that is over for the night, I know tomorrow morning will be easier – he won't be so hard on the kids and me.* But I knew it would be the same the next night.

He would video call me from work and have his genitals out in his hand whilst the cafe was open, he would ask me to do something for him, I would tell him no. I said I hated when he did that, and begged him to stop. He would reply with, 'Fine, plenty of other sluts out there that are far easier than you.'

I was exhausted, I knew I wanted to leave but I didn't know how, he had threatened to cut my mother's head off, he had said that if the kids and I ever left he would burn the house down with us in it.

He was so aggressive towards others, just a nasty person with absolutely no empathy towards anyone.

He was at work seven days a week, but I was paying for everything at home. Food, children's clothing, bills. Hell, I even bought food for his cafe with my money. I helped set up the graphic design work and the website. I was doing everything.

I would occasionally drop my boys off at the cafe so that they could see their dad, I thought they had fun and were learning important life skills.

The boys would come home after I picked them up and say, 'Mama, Baba was so angry. All he does is sit on his phone and order us to work like animals.'

I found out after I had left the relationship that at one point he had tied my three-and-a-half-year-old son up to a chair with a towel at the cafe and threatened him with a knife to shut up otherwise he would kill him. The worst part about this abuse was that he made my thirteen-year-old son perform it. So he had him tie and untie his youngest brother to a chair.

The boys had become desensitised to this behaviour and saw it as normal, they never even told me. I had no idea this was happening, as far as I knew I was the only one being abused and they didn't see it …

The Department for Child Protection were the ones who told me of their abuse, the boys had disclosed during interviews post-separation.

I was being fully abused in every facet of my life – emotionally, mentally, physically, sexually, religiously and financially.

Through that, I tried to be the best of the best at everything I did, I thought my qualifications were going to waste.

I wanted to start a business, just to make a few extra dollars a week so I could buy the kids the things they needed and have a little money for myself to perhaps buy some new clothes.

So I called Jody, as with every major life decision, I always called Jody. I said, 'Jodes, I want to start a business.'

She replied, 'Oh awesome! Another one?'

We both laughed. 'Yes, Jodes, yet another business. I need your help designing a logo.'

Jody is a graphic designer and has helped me with all my great business ideas in the past (none of which ever really worked out).

So she popped over and we got to work on a logo, I pulled out my laptop and started watching YouTube videos on how to build a DIY ecommerce website.

We ate peanut butter sandwiches and mie goreng as we were both broke. We laughed and said to each other, 'Imagine if this actually takes off and we sit back and laugh about how we sat here eating PB sandwiches and held the cord into my broken laptop at a certain angle to stop the battery from dying, that would be hilarious!'

Well, four years on and we do exactly that, the business took off. It became an international brand and sold worldwide.

Through my business, I would sit back and watch other people, especially women, grow their businesses, I would give them the tools with my courses and teach them how to train others to do the same. I thought, *I am helping these women get through tough times and it feels so good!*

But little did I know, that through this it was actually these people, these women that were helping *me*. I started to grow through their growth.

I started to earn money and gain confidence within myself, I started to know who I was and it felt *so damn good.*

I remember driving in the car wearing my scarf on my head and thinking, *God, I just want to feel the wind blow through my long blonde hair, I want to feel the heat from the sunshine on my face and I want the music up so loud I can feel it in my chest.*

So I took my car, I ripped off my scarf, wound down all the windows and cranked up the music and drove.

FREEDOM! Fucking glorious freedom. It felt so good I had goosebumps all over, I had tears in my eyes and I just wanted to scream, 'I'm free!'

But I knew I had to soon cover back up, turn the music down. Turn the car cameras back on and become the 'good wife' and go back home.

But I couldn't help myself from grinning, I knew something my husband didn't. Every time he would push and shove me, yell at me, rape me. I would go to that moment in my head, and I would smile.

He was confused, he started going crazy. He would demand to know why I was so happy and smiling when nothing funny was happening.

I replied with, 'Just because.'

I started to grow very strong and his abuse no longer affected me, I knew my worth and value. I am an extremely strong and valuable woman.

That scared him – the more I grew and became happy with myself. The less emotional reactions I had to his abuse, the more it drove him crazy.

I learnt that he is the weak one, I am the strong one, and all along, for ten years, I was the one feeding him with his emotional supply of all sorts of fucked up.

What I craved all my life was stability, to feel like I mattered. Through my abuse I found out that I had it all along.

That abusers needed it to feel powerful, to feel in control. You see, victims of domestic violence are not weak. We are the strongest people you will ever know.

We have so much value and power that an abuser needs us to function, they literally can't function unless we feed them with what exists inside of us.

I discovered that I was the source of my value and I didn't need a partner to have structure and stability. *I can do that myself*, was the most liberating self-realisation moment I have ever had in my life.

I woke up on 3 January 2020 and went to the bathroom as per usual. I noticed my husband's phone on the bathroom counter. He never left his phone around, it was always locked with a PIN I never knew and it was one of many phones.

I never knew anything about him, how much he earned per week, who his friends were. He made me hide out the back of the cafe if his mates turned up.

So it immediately grabbed my attention, the night before, by pure luck, I had seen him enter the PIN out the corner of my eye.

I just picked up the phone and opened the text messages, I wasn't searching for anything in particular but if your husband has hidden his phones away from you for ten years, I mean, a girl is curious.

WELL, BANG! There was text after text to sex workers, asking when he could meet them, how much for certain acts he wanted done, where he could meet them.

They were dated, on my birthday, when my youngest son was in hospital extremely ill.

I felt my heart in my ears, I could hear myself breathing, it was like my next steps were in slow motion.

The bathroom door. *Bang-bang-bang* It's him. 'Unlock this door now!' I opened the door with his phone in my hand. He stops in complete silence.

Now I wish this had been caught on camera, this was the ultimate switch. Like a movie scene – in that moment, I took back all my power. I got angry, it was like my life flashed before my eyes.

I thought, *How dare he? How dare he treat me like this for years on end? I sacrificed everything – my friends, family, body, career and my self for him.* Then this, it was a complete and utter deep-seated knowing that it was over. It felt like complete relief and freedom.

I said to him, phone in hand, 'Explain this.'

He said, 'Oh, you know why I did it.'

Then I agreed and said, 'Yes, I do. Because you are a weak and insecure man. Our marriage is over and I will no longer be your wife or your property. You can pack your bags and leave immediately.'

I think he was in so much shock that I actually finally stood up for myself, he thought I was joking.

He went off to work and tried to guilt-trip me into feeling bad for him.

But I felt free, I finally found my out and he handed it to me on a golden platter.

He came back to the house later that night, with the intention of seeing the children. I allowed it, I was all for co-parenting. I wasn't going to be a mother who kept the children away from their dad.

But what followed, changed everything.

He came back to the house with a knife, he had lost control. He walked to the boys' bedroom with a kitchen knife and told them to say goodbye to him forever and look after each other.

Then he went to the master bedroom, I followed and closed the door behind me. I didn't want the children to see him if he did anything.

I said, 'I'm calling 000, you need help.' He begged me not to, but I thought he needed professional help. I thought an ambulance would take him off to the hospital and assess him and everything would be okay.

But the police turned up, they placed him in the back of a paddy wagon and issued me with a seventy-two-hour police restraining order.

I was tired and confused, I messaged my girlfriends and said *Happy New Year to me! My husband has been cheating on me with prostitutes and just came into the house with a knife, the police have taken him. LOL*

That was my normal ... no-one else knew, I was so used to his behaviour I didn't realise the severity of it or even label myself as being in a domestic violence relationship.

My girlfriends were like, *WTF?! Nicole we will be at your place in ten mins,* then all five of them turned up in their PJs and sat with me while the police took my statement and then they started to take over.

My friend and the policeman said, 'Nicole, you are in a domestic violence relationship. We don't know the severity of it because you have kept it so well hidden.'

I started vomiting into my front garden bed, the shock of what happened hit me. It was blurry after that, my friends wrote lists of what to do – who was watching the kids.

We had police at the house almost every night, running

through escape plans, DCP interviews and court cases. It was overwhelming.

I had a restraining order put in place which he officially breached twice – many more times actually, but it was not able to be proven, I was stalked and a tracker was placed on my car. My friends were stalked and I was absolutely terrified for mine and my children's lives.

At the same time, you are trying to parent through trauma, keep food on the table and do your own healing.

It was exhausting. But I went to the groups, got therapy, kept focused on my business and my kids, and kept strong for them. The boys now would be looking for stability and structure and comfort and I had that. I *AM* that.

I want to show them that no matter what happens in life, we all have the power and value to get through the hardest trials.

I wanted them to know that when they are men, that no-one has the right to make you feel you are less than what you are. No-one has the right to make you feel like you don't matter.

You have rights and you don't need to take them from anyone else.

I wanted to author this piece in *Love, Bruises & Bullsh!t* as a tribute to my beautiful nana who passed away on 4 October 2019. I hope you're proud of me now, Nana, the cycle ends here.

I hope this, as well as the other stories in this powerful book, inspires and moves you, to be that change you wish to see in the world.

Confused

CONFUSED.
Danni

I was a confident and adventurous twenty-one-year-old with a one-way ticket to New Zealand to fulfil my dreams of spending a year travelling and working abroad. It was a summer's night in late January, and I had just met this handsome and charming young man. After a couple of drinks and a long conversation about ourselves, I shared my plans with him. I wasn't looking to date anyone at this time. It was like a romance movie unfolding before me when he told me I was the kind of girl he would be willing to wait for. No-one had ever empowered me like that before, and I felt so special and appreciated. I had moved out of my rental and sold a lot of my belongings, including my car. Most of my possessions fit into a couple of suitcases, and my journey was just about to begin.

Over the next four weeks, we started quickly and officially dating. He picked me up in a new ute on our first date and took me to a nice restaurant. I wouldn't say the date went overly well. The conversation didn't flow and I wasn't feeling any sparks, but he appeared to be a regular guy with genuine interest. After the date he told me how much he enjoyed my company, and how amazingly confident and hardworking I was. On our second date, he picked me up in a different, older car with a snapped antenna. He admitted he had borrowed the nicer-looking car, he wanted to impress me because he thought I was out of his league. He also told me that he had a one-year-old daughter to a spiteful woman who would lie and restrict his access to his baby. He would tell stories of how she would message him saying he could see the baby, but then she would change her mind. I felt sorry for this kind and caring dad I was starting to really like. His childhood hadn't been a happy one and he was estranged from most of his family. The maternal instinct in me felt like he was someone who needed my love, care and protection.

He told me I should follow my dreams, and no matter how long I was gone, he would be waiting when I returned home. He would tell me that I was amazing, kind, generous, loving to my friends and family, and I was the type of woman he would love to settle down with and have children. After only after a short time, he made me undoubtedly believe I was the best thing that had ever come into his life. We would speak daily, and he had fallen in love with me. I was starting to envision my childhood dreams of being a loving mother and doting housewife coming true.

While at home spending time with him I received a Facebook message from his ex-girlfriend warning me. Our relationship wasn't public on social media, but she found me and made it clear that he had been abusive towards her and attached photos of her bruises. He had explained that she was manipulative, crazy and abusive, and he was the victim in their relationship. He previously cried tears to me over how she was keeping his child from him for no reason. When I told him I had received that message, he broke down crying, emphasising that she was a liar and accused her of making things up. He seemed so gentle that I couldn't imagine him ever emotionally or physically hurting someone. There was no reason to stop seeing him. The couple of weeks before my trip felt so perfect.

My New Zealand trip came up fast and off I went. I intended to spend the first few weeks holidaying with a friend, who was then returning home while I stayed on and lived for a while. I enjoyed myself but still thought of this guy who had forged a space in my feelings. He kept telling me how much he missed me and couldn't wait until I returned home, but understood that I was following my dreams. In the end, I decided that I would not stay and work. I thought if I stayed any longer, I could miss the opportunity of being with someone who genuinely wanted to be with me. While I was gone, he and a close friend of mine had both needed to move house and decided they should rent together. When I returned home with my few possessions and suitcase, I moved in with him. I didn't have a car and was looking for work, so we spent a lot of time together. In only three short months, one month of which I wasn't even in the country, I had fallen in love with someone I thought could be the one.

Slowly he began to alienate me from my friends and family. The friend of mine that had been living with him moved out after a couple of months because she didn't like his behaviour. There had been instances when they disagreed about things, and she had come to not like his attitude and manner. He would tell me his side of the story where he was the 'victim', and I kept making excuses for him. One day when I wasn't home, they disagreed about something and his reaction was so overblown that he yelled, slamming a frying pan so hard against the tiles that the frying pan bent. He told me he had a terrible day, and his ex-girlfriend had again denied him the right to see his daughter. When he flipped out it was a reaction to that, not the situation. He believed the frying pan must have been cheap because he didn't hit the wall that hard. To this point, he had given me no reason to doubt him, and I reasoned that their personalities just clashed.

On a rare social evening we invited my closest two girlfriends and their partners over for dinner and drinks. After having dinner and a few drinks we heard music coming from across the road. He suggested we go over there, investigate and potentially join in. I thought it was odd but he was set on going over there, and so I followed him. My friends thought it was weird that we would want to go to the neighbours' when we were having fun, so they stayed at our house. The neighbours' garage door was slightly up and we could tell it was a teenagers' party. I began insisting that we turn around and go home because it obviously wasn't a party for us. He forged right ahead and knocked on the door. The father of the teenagers answered and suddenly a switch went off. He started hurling abuse at the man saying, 'What the fuck are you making so much noise for? This is a family suburb! We have a baby sleeping over the road and you need to shut the fuck up!' I remember being very confused as this was a complete lie, there were no children at our house. The man told him to leave while shutting the front door and the garage, but in a rage while leaving the property, my boyfriend hit the garage door so hard that it dented. When we got back my friends tried to intervene and calm him down. This didn't go well and he threw a four-pack of premixed bourbon straight at their heads, smashing glass and alcohol all over the walls and floor. My friends had already called the police by this point and when the police arrived, I told them everything was okay and they could leave. My friends were worried and tried to make me leave with them, but he had gone to another room and was sobbing, saying he was sorry and, 'I am so ashamed of myself.' He needed me and begged me to stay.

The next day was followed by more sobbing and apologising. He was angry because he thought my friends didn't include him, he felt like an outsider and didn't think he was good enough for me.

According to him, all those reasons combined with the drinking was what led to the outburst. He framed it as it was us – me and him – against the world.

We appeared to the outside world as a quiet couple, content in each other's company, who didn't socialise much. He didn't have any friends or hobbies. Most of the time he was home he would be playing on gaming devices or watching movies. I had become more reclusive and didn't see much of my friends. It seemed either he didn't like them or they didn't like him. On the odd occasion I did see them he said it was taking valuable time away from us and I always felt guilty. He made me feel like it was wrong for having photos of ex-boyfriends in photo albums, so I went through and threw them all out. When it came to social media, particularly Facebook, he said it was unnecessary and it was only used for attracting a partner or spying on other people's lives. He maintained that we didn't need to do either of those things and that we didn't want anyone to be doing those things to us. Facebook accounts were just trouble, so I deleted mine. When I did what he wanted he made me think it was my idea, showering me in compliments and praise reinforcing my compliance. It seemed to prove that he knew me better than I knew myself.

He wanted to see his daughter, but he didn't know how to achieve that. On one occasion he went to his ex's house and demanded he have her overnight. He had been successful in bringing his daughter home, but he was bleeding from scratches on his leg. When I questioned him he said his 'crazy' ex had pushed him through a glass table. That night when the baby was crying and unsettled, he broke down, saying he didn't know how to be a father because he had been robbed of that experience by his ex. After he took his daughter home the next day, his ex said she wouldn't let him see his daughter anymore and that if he wanted to see her, he could apply through the family courts. I felt so sorry for him. He insisted that he was not intelligent enough to understand the way the system worked so I did all the legwork. I helped him figure out how he could get visitation by making some phone calls. Finally, when we did get visitation for him, it was supervised. He said he couldn't do supervised visits because it was too emotionally hard for him and being unable to see his daughter broke his heart. I wasn't allowed to babysit my best friend's daughter because it reminded him of his own daughter. This broke my heart as I considered her daughter almost as my own – but I gave his feelings priority over my own.

He had made some poor financial decisions in the past, and because we were living together, suggested I should manage our finances. He insisted that he wanted to look after me and our future, but the truth was we didn't have enough income to pay the rent, debts and general living costs. I was working part-time and had just re-enrolled at university to continue the degree that I put on hold for my overseas adventure. Once it became clear that we had to make budget cuts, he switched from being supportive and happy to giving criticism and blame. He insisted that I must be spending too much and was being selfish going back to university when we needed me to work full-time. He was spending money we did not have and if I ever questioned a purchase or insisted we didn't have the funds, he would tell me he earned more than enough for us to live and that it was my problem to figure out. To sustain our life together, I got a full-time job. He pushed me to negotiate my roles and responsibilities in this job, such as changing my working hours to ensure I would be home to cook dinner. The money pressure eased, but the denial of my true authentic self increased.

I tried to help him get out of debt, completed all the general life paperwork and bill-paying, I drove when he didn't have his licence, I advocated for him to see his daughter and I provided him with emotional support. However, I rarely did any of these things well enough to his standard, and I was constantly walking on eggshells striving to please him. The house had to be run exactly to his liking. I had to buy fresh bread rolls daily to make his lunch because he didn't like eating bread that was a few days old. If, for any reason, I hadn't got the rolls or I hadn't finished making dinner by the time he expected it, he would yell that I was useless and couldn't be depended on. If I tried to leave the house to escape the yelling, he would grab me or push me so I physically couldn't leave. I didn't know when he came home each day if he would be happy, or if there would be something that would set him off. If the house was sparkling clean he would pick on the fact that I hadn't folded the bedsheets with perfect hospital corners. He would tell me that I was terrible at cleaning and I shouldn't bother, or alternatively, he would make me do it over.

I had lost a lot of weight in the nine months we had been dating. He told me it was because I was happy and in love, and I was so sexy. According to him, I had improved so much since we got together. He would buy me presents, always knowing the most thoughtful and perfect gift, capturing EXACTLY what I wanted. In October 2010, he took me out to a fancy dinner that he had pre-booked. It had been a long day and I just wanted to stay home, but he was very insistent. After abnormally quickly scoffing down his meal, he got down on one knee and asked me to marry him. He had been so meticulous in asking my father, notifying the waitstaff and organising a beautiful bottle of champagne. He had done all the 'right' things. The next morning, rather than feeling swooned and excited, I felt sick to my stomach, I knew I shouldn't be marrying him but I didn't know how to get out of it. And as is the case in many emotionally manipulative relationships, I didn't always want to get out of it.

It was the early hours of New Year's Day when I received a call notifying me that he was hit by a police car and had been hospitalised. The night before we had been at my best friend's New Year's Eve party. We never usually went to social gatherings together, but I was trying to reconnect with my friends, so we did. Around 10/11pm he became aggressive with me because I had failed to let him know that my ex-boyfriend's cousin also lived at my best friend's house, and that my ex's brother was also at the party. I lived in this house before going to New Zealand, and this was my main friendship group. We had a verbal disagreement, and he disappeared. After a while, I called and texted, but there was no response. At 4am my mother had to come pick me up to take me to the hospital. The next day followed with lots of upset and disappointment directed at both himself and me. The cycle was always the same – get triggered, flip out, blame me, get sad, blame me and the situation/circumstances/his background, insist that he needs me. And repeat.

We tried again to go to a social gathering in late January for the birthday of one of my close work friends. We sat at a table mostly apart from the crowd and we didn't mingle. After a while, for no reason, he snarled at me, 'What the fuck do you think you're doing?' I was taken aback, I didn't realise I was doing anything. I was simply sitting having a drink and I hadn't even spoken to many people (hard for someone who is naturally a mingler). He accused me of looking at a guy who was standing at the bar. I hadn't even noticed him before my fiancé had, and he started harassing me with a barrage of questions like, 'Who is he? Why are you looking at him? Why do you need to look at other men? We're engaged. What do you do when I'm not around if this is what you do right in front of me?' Of course, after that, the afternoon was ruined and we left. The whole ride home I was interrogated. The middle-aged male accountant from my work was also a target of his belligerent behaviour. In discussing our works days one evening I relayed a story about this man from work. My boyfriend accused me of having an affair or having an unhealthy obsession with him, saying I always talked about him. I don't think his name had ever come up before – and he was an older man that I just happened to work with and talk to that day.

On another day of walking on eggshells I decided I would take a walk around the block. My fiancé was in a state about something and had retreated to playing video games. As I walked past him and let him know I was going on a walk he instantly flipped. He was convinced I was going to call my mum and best friend and get them to come and get me, and that they'd make me leave him. When I tried to reassure him he told me he could see my phone in my pocket and I wouldn't need a phone if I was just going for a walk – I must have some ulterior motive. I continued to deny his accusations and he threw a drinking glass at me, which hit my arm and then smashed on the ground, taking another chip out of the tiles that had been subject to many thrown objects. I distinctly remember after that incident, feeling the pain and seeing the visible bruise on my arm, that I needed a way to escape. As I had many times before, I told myself that the next time he flipped over nothing, or the next time he grabbed or pushed me or threw something at me, I would leave. This was the last time I would put up with it. Alas, the cycle continued and I didn't keep that promise to myself.

In March 2011, fourteen months after our first meeting, he was jailed for assault. He had begun seeing a lawyer about six months prior, and had explained that he was being charged for assaulting an off-duty police officer. The assault had happened a couple of months before we'd met, and he'd always framed it in a way that made him look like a victim. The judge, before handing down sentencing, explained that due to the TWO prior assault convictions he would be receiving an eighteen-month sentence. He had never disclosed to me that he had prior charges of any kind and I was completely blindsided. At that moment I realised I barely knew this man at all. After he was remanded in custody I went straight to my best friend's house and felt a wave of relief as it was the first time I could freely speak about how I felt and the things that had been going on without fear of repercussions. I also felt a strong guilt as I realised how much I had neglected and negated the relationships and people that mattered to me and that genuinely cared about me. The night before the hearing my grandfather had passed away. For the months prior I was unable to see my grandfather because I was supporting my fiancé during these uncertain times. My mother also had spent the week supporting me in court rather than being with her family grieving her father's death.

The hold he had on me was strong, and despite the instant relief, it still took me another few weeks and several psychologist visits to break things off with him. It also wasn't until this time that I knew what had been going on with his ex and daughter. He had always maintained to me that she was preventing him access. Once he was in jail I went through his phone and saw she was being much more accommodating and that it was mostly him who was changing plans and not following through. I packed up his belongings, put them into storage and started rebuilding my life. The fact that he was in prison gave me a sense of safety and security that I hadn't experienced in a long time, but I was still nervous thinking forward to how he might react once he was released. A year later I seized an opportunity to relocate half way around the world, my way of escaping him and knowing he couldn't find me.

> **TO THIS DAY, WHEN SHARING MY STORY, I STILL FEEL THE NEED TO JUSTIFY HIS OUTLANDISH AND ABUSIVE ACTIONS, JUST AS HE JUSTIFIED THEM TO ME. IF YOU RECOGNISE THESE TRAITS IN YOUR PARTNER/S IT IS IMPORTANT TO KNOW YOU CANNOT FIX THEM, BUT YOU CAN LOOK AFTER YOURSELF AND YOUR NEEDS. DESPITE NOT FITTING THE MAINSTREAM IDEA OF A TYPICAL 'DOMESTIC ABUSE VICTIM', THE EMOTIONAL PAIN FROM THE MANIPULATION AND COERCIVE CONTROL, EVEN AFTER TEN YEARS, HAS CONTINUED TO IMPACT MY EVERYDAY LIFE.**

Stuck!

STUCK.
Tanya

A brief about my story that makes it different – perhaps – I am writing about psychological abuse. I did not know it even existed until I discovered that I had been subjected to it for fifteen years – and yet I didn't know!

My abuse took place in my head, it is unseen and so very hard for others to believe, even those closest to me. It took place very slowly and steadily over a long period of time.

I would like my story told in the hope it may help another or even alert someone else to what is going on in their own life so that they do not experience what I did or so they can get out or seek help for their situation.

I would like to tell you my story.

I would like to tell it to you in the hope it may help someone else gain confirmation of what they went through. Perhaps someone will recognise the signs and get out of a similar relationship and I really hope after someone reads this, they will avoid ever ending up in the same situation I did.

I would also like to share my story as I never ever thought something like this could happen to me. I never thought anything like this existed or was even possible to do to someone, yet it was possible and it did happen to me.

I was always a very independent female. I grew up believing that there was more to life than getting married and having children. I wasn't sure what I was searching for but I set about fulfilling all of my dreams. I set goals and I achieved them. If I said I was doing something, I did it.

By the time I met my abuser I had lived in three different countries, travelled to a huge list of my favourite destinations, I was following a spiritual path, was very fit and healthy, owned a property and a car, and I believed anything was possible.

When I finally managed to escape him I no longer knew what was real, I didn't believe I was even likeable, my husband had made it very clear there was nothing I could do right. I knew that there was nothing good he could say about me as a wife. I was wracked with fear and insecurities, I had no self-belief, no ability to say 'no' – there was nothing left of me as a person. I felt destroyed down to a soul level. I felt terrified and I reacted to anything and everything, it seemed. I specifically remember feeling like a cloud was being lifted from my head after I had some time away from him. I was so confused. Confusion had been my norm for almost fifteen years … as had fear.

I was also unable to cook anything. There was like an invisible wall that I just couldn't get past when it came to cooking. I would walk aimlessly around the supermarket unable to choose food for dinner. I had the same food for myself every single day. My daughter had the same meals every week on the same days. I was unable to break out of whatever prison I was in, regarding being able to create a culinary delight, yet I had loved creating new dishes and trying new recipes.

So how did that happen to me?

I met my abuser at a rock climbing gym. I had placed an advert for a partner to climb with. He called me, we met and I thought he was lovely! My stomach did a flip when I first met him … I thought that was a sign … it was – a warning sign!

We climbed together regularly. He fascinated the hell out of me, mainly because he was so different to me. He was dark and quiet, I thought he was shy. He didn't talk much and I would ramble on sharing all about myself. I would charge up the rock but he would look, and slowly make moves.

After three months I set off to England to begin more travelling. I was away for two years and he stayed in touch. He knew I was interested in spiritual and philosophical books and he would send me emails about things he'd read. This really hooked me in and I thought, *I'm falling for this guy and I haven't even kissed him,* I certainly had not experienced that before.

I returned to Australia, he'd bought a house with his girlfriend, I thought that was a very serious thing to do, so accepted that we were only going to be friends. His relationship fell apart within a matter of months and he made it very clear he was interested in me.

I told him to go and have some fun first and then come and see me. I said I did not want to be his rebound chick.

He needed a place to live so he moved in with my friend. He had a suitcase of clothes and

> **SUCCESS IS NOT MEASURED BY WHAT A PERSON ACCOMPLISHED, BUT BY THE OPPOSITION THEY HAVE ENCOUNTERED, AND THE COURAGE WITH WHICH THEY HAVE MAINTAINED THE STRUGGLE AGAINST THE ODDS. – JOE SARAH**

a car that needed pushing to get it going. He also had lots of stories about his ex-girlfriend, how unfairly he was treated by her family and that she had a temper on her … (warning sign).

Despite me telling him to go elsewhere first, we very quickly ended up out at a bar and I went back to my friend's to sleep (where he was living). I was adamant I would not sleep with him straight away as I wanted to 'have my eyes wide open'. My belief was, as women, we get emotionally involved once we have sex, and it clouds our vision when it comes to men. I wanted to make sure I made the right choice and did not get involved with someone I was not well suited to.

That night he came and jumped on the couch where I was sleeping. He suggested that we take off all of our clothes and just lay next to each other and then I could see that I could trust him (warning sign). I wasn't keen but he had this way of being able to talk me into anything. I didn't get naked but I did get down to my knickers and we just kissed.

One thing that shocked me was on that very first night of 'getting together' he said, 'So are you going to be the mother of my children?' I was shocked. I wasn't thinking that far ahead at all (warning sign).

My story is very hard to put into words. I suffered a form of abuse that was very slow and subtle. Psychological abuse for almost fifteen years. Abuse that messes with your mind, your brain, your beliefs, your world view, your confidence, your self-belief.

He chose me purposely as he could see that I was someone he could do this to. I was kind, caring, giving and always considered other people. I put other people before myself and felt too bad to speak up about a lot of things. I also had a house and car and was good with money.

From the first meal I cooked him he criticised me, or rather, mocked my cooking. He would make out as if it was a joke that he was making – but it wasn't. I was a vegetarian and him a meat eater. I have no idea as to why I thought it would work! I felt terrible about the food I cooked him and set about trying to please him. For the first two years or so I cooked all of his traditional South American food. He was happy when I did that, however when I realised that I wanted some of the food *I* liked, problems arose. He just would not eat the food that I loved. I specifically remember him scraping his plate of food into the bin in front of me.

As time wore on and I had my daughter, I would get excited trialling new dishes only to have her say, 'Yuck,' and then he would join in with her and neither of them ate my food. My sense of failure at not being able to cook, grew so much that I just stopped cooking for him. I would leave his food out and he would cook it when he got in from work.

From the very beginning he never seemed to have any money and constantly confirmed this to me. It was like he was brainwashing me as he just kept repeating this story to me over and over. He ran his own business and then began teaching whilst others worked for him, yet he constantly said there was no money. He didn't want to go away on holiday due to lack of funds, we had old cars and old phones. Every term he would tell me the teaching work was dying off and he didn't have many classes, yet he always worked six days a week.

When I look back, it just does not make sense how he could work so much and yet not have any money, but at the time I did not have that clarity.

One thing that did regularly appear were his debts – mainly tax debts – he just would not pay enough tax and debt collectors would come looking for him. The other debt was parking fines. He would park his car but not purchase a ticket and so the fines arrived weekly.

He would only share his teaching money with me and the family so there was no income from him over the Christmas holidays. I had no idea about his business and how much money he was making there. The lack of regular income made me constantly feel on edge and I developed a fear of finances which I cannot explain as I had never had it before. If ever I asked him about his business finances something else would always pop up so he could avoid going through them with me. On the few occasions I did manage to get him to show me his accounts he got scarily angry and I became too scared to ask to see his accounts.

He happily moved in with me into my house in Scarborough and then set his sights on upscaling. He encouraged me to put all of our spendings onto the Visa card in my name to earn Frequent Flyer points. We did not have joint accounts at any time.

At that time I was in love with him and believed he was my 'special one'. I wanted to get married. He was not so keen. I thought this was because his parents were divorced. I received a payout from my work and suggested we elope. We had a ring made at a jeweller that knew him through his business. Three of us chose a top-quality diamond and studied it through the eyeglass.

We got married in the Maldives and the day after the wedding I looked at my ring and noticed a black dot in the diamond. It was so large it could be seen easily. I knew this was not the diamond we had chosen. This caused me an enormous amount of anxiety and I went to see the jewellers as soon as we returned. They could not explain it. My new husband had the ring in his possession for the week preceding the wedding. This was just the beginning of many unusual 'occurrences'.

It was not until after I had received significant EMDR therapy that my memory began to return and I was able to recall the very special items of mine that had 'disappeared':

- My video of white water rafting the Zambezi River (I'd told him that was my greatest achievement)
- A model troll from New Zealand (a very special gift from a friend)
- Special photos and memorabilia from my travels
- My jewellery bag after a stay at a hotel (later found under the bathroom sink)
- My sewing kit (which I found stashed in the study cupboard after I had searched extensively for it)
- The coffee pot we took on holiday just vanished from the car (yet I got blamed for leaving it behind)
- My favourite clothes disappeared and my underwear (I would find these hidden in his drawers)
- My meditation CDs

The list was endless.

My ruby and diamond ring inherited from my grandmother and another beautiful diamond ring disappeared from our house one day when I rushed out to work. I had left them behind accidentally and they were never seen again. I asked him to help me look for them but he walked straight past me as if I had said nothing. By that stage I doubted myself so much I thought I had lost them at work, who knows how.

This is a very specific form of psychological abuse that causes you to doubt yourself. I always seemed to lose things. Sometimes I would ask him for help and he would find the things that I couldn't. I began believing I was stupid and I became the family joke.

The most heartbreaking loss was on holiday at Coral Bay when we were doing some rock climbing, I asked him to look after my rings as they were getting scratched. I had my grandmother's wedding ring and my own. He placed them into his pockets. He rock climbed and then ran over and started doing sit-ups madly on the beach. I thought it was strange and just watched him. I then noticed my wedding ring in the sand as it had fallen out of his pocket. Unfortunately, I forgot about the ring in the other pocket – my grandmother's wedding ring that I wore. I was so heartbroken that I searched for days in the sand whilst crying my eyes out. He just got nasty and said it wasn't his fault.

Another favourite trick of his was to deny that I had told him things. This went on for fifteen years, and believe me, this leaves you confused. I would tell him our social plans and yet when it came to the date he would claim to know nothing about it, but I knew I'd told him. Then he would say that he had told me things when I knew he hadn't. Some specific moments were so blatant – I told him I read something in the newspaper. 'No you didn't,' he told me. I told him I wanted my daughter to spend less time on her iPad. He agreed and then walked over to her and gave it to her right in front of me.

He liked to treat me like I did not exist. He would not speak to me, just my daughter, he would sit and watch TV – just with her, and cook dinner just for her. He would make me sit in the back of the car and she got the front seat. They would go out together and if I went to join them I was told to 'go away'. By the end of the marriage I felt like I had no relationship with my daughter and yet she was only ten years of age at the time.

His nastiness towards me was completely random. I had no idea when it would surface. He was a complete Jekyll and Hyde character. We were heading home one New Year's Eve and completely out of the blue he said, 'I give us six months.' I had no idea what he was talking about. Another year on my birthday we had a lovely night out for dinner yet when we got home he declared, 'That's it, we're done, only YOU'RE moving out this time.' I was very upset. Nothing had even happened. I have a long list of such occurrences all happening on what I considered special days – birthdays, Christmas etc.

He would contrast this nastiness with buying me fabulous birthday and Christmas gifts and randomly surprising me with a lovely meal. This made me doubt my opinion of him.

I found myself constantly doing things around the house just so that he would not be horrible to me. I never seemed to sit down and was unable to relax. I was constantly on edge, never knowing when he would be nasty.

I tried my best with presents for him but he just did not seem to like anything I bought him. I felt like a failure. He did not stick with any interests or stand by any of his so-called beliefs, so that I did not know who he was. All I knew was that nothing I did was good enough. I also knew that no matter how wonderful I was, it fell on blind eyes – he saw no good in me and there was not an ounce of appreciation for me being his wife and mum to our daughter.

I discovered I was pregnant six months into our marriage. His response was, 'Oh shit. Let's not talk about it or we won't be able to sleep.' I was upset and crying and asked for some reassurance. He said, 'Oh come on, Tanya, you know you'll be fine.' I felt alone. He would not come near me as the pregnancy wore on. He complained I was 'big down there'. I shared that I wanted a caesarean. His response was, 'Surely you can have at least one child naturally!' There was no support.

I had my daughter and he spent time at the hospital watching the TV. I did not receive flowers from him. I wondered why he was there. When I came home from hospital, there was nothing in the house. The first thing I had to do was go to the shops with my caesarean stitches and a newborn in tow.

He began criticising me as a mother as soon as my daughter was born. I had no idea what I was doing – I'd never been a mum before and yet he constantly questioned me. I felt like a failure and yet I had the most wonderful child, that was the envy of other mothers, as she slept so well.

I had to return to casual work almost immediately as he did not support us financially and then, when my daughter was one year of age, another tax debt arrived. I felt so worried that I set about finding part-time work. I ended up as the primary provider for the family on my part-time income. I knew I could not rely on him financially and this created enormous stress and worry. I lived in constant fear of how we would survive.

When I look back at my marriage I realise it was a series of cycles that I went through. The cycle would begin with some revelation by him that would ultimately destroy me emotionally. I would try to end it but he would then set about attempting to repair things. Then there would be the next revelation to destroy me. Sorry was not a word he used. He would only ever say, 'I apologise.'

I tried to get away from him but I honestly felt like I had hooks in me attached to my stomach. No matter how hard I tried, he was always able to pull me back in. I now know that this is called a trauma bond.

These were the cycles I went through:

In 2008 (when my daughter was eighteen months old) he asked me to get something from his bag. There were only two items in his bag – the thing he asked me to get and a bank loan book. He had a bank loan (at a bank I didn't know of) that was over five years, according to the booklet. I confronted him and he said it was for only two thousand dollars but it was closer to ten thousand. He cried and begged me to forgive him. He convinced me it was for a debt from before we were married. I used the equity from my house to pay off the debt for him. I do not believe my discovery of his debt was an accident. He did not say sorry or attempt to make it up to me in any way. He just carried on with life as if nothing had happened when I was broken. At that stage I decided not to have any more children with him as I began to think we wouldn't make it.

In 2009, exactly a year later, we were heading out and got pulled over by the police. I discovered that he had lost his driving licence six months beforehand, for unpaid parking fines. I was in shock and couldn't believe he was lying again. We separated for a short time. He seemed unphased, smiled, took the laptop and headed off – leaving me heartbroken.

He began talking about me having another child – only it wasn't a friendly chat. I specifically remember feeling like I was being bullied into it. He said, 'What's wrong with you? Every other woman wants to have children but not you! You haven't got a maternal bone in your body.' Nowhere did he explain how we would survive financially if we had another child.

In 2010, exactly a year after the last revelation, I discovered that he had been to see an ex-girlfriend in Sydney. He had been very strange with me and wouldn't kiss me and was secretive with his phone. He blamed me and said I was scared to have another child with him. I found emails between the two of them and confronted him. He blamed me further saying, 'There are reasons why men have affairs, you know!' If ever I mentioned it he would say, 'Oh God you're not still going on about that are you?'

This incident took a lot longer to repair and we attended couples therapy and he even proposed to me again. I thought we were back on track to where we should be at that stage in our marriage. We had a summer holiday and then one day I went to the letterbox and discovered a Visa card debt from a bank we didn't have an account at. This was January 2013. The letter had been redirected from his work address. I do believe it was him that redirected it.

I knew this debt could not be from before we met and I demanded to know what it was for. He sat at the table in front of me and casually told me that he had been seeing escorts since before we were married (we were still having sex four times a week at that stage). He also told me he was addicted to online porn, porn shops and that he had watched porn on the college computers where he taught! He then walked off. I was left literally unable to speak, and that revelation broke me on a whole other level.

I am unable to put into words the horror and disgust I felt at him being able to look me in the eyes and lie, knowing that we would have had sex after he had been with a prostitute, knowing that I had given my beautiful daughter such a disgusting father. I honestly have no idea how I made it through that year. I do know that I was at the point of suicide three times. It was not because I wanted to die, I just did not want this to be my life.

He organised a surprise birthday party for me at a local bar as if everything was fine.

He refused to leave the house and moved upstairs with my daughter and just carried on life as normal. He would get quite angry at me being upset and would have rages and throw things. One time I had to lock him in the garden as I was so scared. He set about openly telling me that he was 'turned on by other women', and when I complained, he answered, 'See, I knew I couldn't tell you.' He felt pleased he was being honest with me but I just could not cope hearing all of the details of him being with other women.

My trauma was such that I became convinced that he was going to kill me. I was terrified of him. One morning he asked to talk with me in the laundry and as he pulled the door closed I knew it would happen then. I just put my hands over my eyes and begged, 'Please don't kill me! Please don't kill me!' This is one of the only times I felt that he listened to me.

I had to ask my dad to help remove him from the house to allow me to recover, but he would still return to the house when I was out and I would find him there. I began suffering flashbacks to things I'd never witnessed (namely him being with prostitutes), I was unable to watch any movie with a sex scene or even a love scene. I set about finding therapy but didn't recognise the extent of the trauma I had suffered.

I now know my coping mechanism is denial. I was able to bury what happened somehow and continue. I think this was all I could do. He kept telling me that I would not survive financially without him. I did not have the strength to leave him and deal with what he had told me at the same time. It was too much. I am amazed that I am still here today.

He booked a family holiday to Japan for three weeks staying at all of the top hotels and visiting Disneyland. He bought us skiing clothes and supplied the spending money. All of this was done on the money that he was keeping to himself. He treated me dreadfully whilst we were away and every day he told me I was wrong about what I had said. Then my daughter started telling me I was wrong too, that's when I spoke up about his behaviour.

He enrolled us in Imago – a couple's course – learning how to communicate. I highly recommend it (for any normal relationship). Part of it is learning to listen to the other person and offer them empathy. My whole body told me he was lying to me with his words of empathy and I just had no wish to offer him empathy in return, after what I had been through with him, and still no apology. I was totally spent emotionally. I had nothing left to give. He complained that I had no empathy and blamed me for our problems (I know now that I am in fact an empath!).

The final straw was when I returned from my life-saving trip to complete the Camino de Santiago (an 800km walk across Spain). This trip saved me and gave me the clarity to escape the hell I was stuck in. He had encouraged me to go and even suggested I stay away for longer.

I returned to a very strange situation, he wouldn't kiss me despite sending me mountains of loving messages whilst I was away. After a few hours of sleep he opened the curtains and ordered me out of bed to go and look after my daughter but she wasn't even up. He began limiting the money for shopping and telling me what I could and couldn't buy, he emptied my savings account. I had no idea what was going on but his treatment towards me was horrendous. He came to see me at my work and he was so awful I hid in the cupboard with my hands over my ears as I just could not take any more. Another time I was driving the car and he began mocking me. I stopped at the lights. He was so awful to me I jumped out of the car and ran, I had no idea where I was. I no longer wanted to return home. He would threaten to tell my parents that we were separating as I was sleeping in my daughter's bedroom. I had also found my wardrobe door open and my jewellery box open, and evidence of drug taking was left on show. He wanted me to know what he had been up to.

My friend was unavailable and yet my daughter told me she had been at her house the whole time I was away. It was clear he was having sex with her. He denied anything was going on but when I went to see her she happily told me they had a 'connection' and that he had asked her to be his 'bedwarmer'. He messed with my mind so much I didn't know what was real and wasn't, I didn't even know if I was in my own house. The two of them were enjoying playing games with my life. He told me he wanted to 'reconnect' with me. He got on his knees in front of me and swore there was nothing going on with him and my friend, yet she told her children that he was in love with her and her children told my daughter.

The best thing I did was to get a restraining order against him. He would not leave me alone, one day he would be nice buying me flowers and chocolates and the next day he would act like he was scared of me in front of my daughter. I had no idea what was going on.

The restraining order gave me some distance from him which is what I needed. With psychological abuse they are in your head and I was terrified of him. I do not know why. My garden was constantly entered as I would find the padlock off the gate, my lights were cut, a branch broken off a tree at the side of my house, I would get up and the car door would be open. It is very hard to get anyone to believe you about what you are experiencing or the fear that you have. He breached the restraining order multiple times yet the police would not act until I had been there three times. They did not think his breaches were bad enough.

He began court action to gain custody of my daughter. I had to attend mediation and yet I was in no fit state to do so. The mediators have no understanding of someone suffering the repercussions of abuse. I was a complete mess and I do not think the mediator believed what I said to him.

My husband's affidavit in family court was complete lies. He accused me of abusing him and threatening to harm myself and my daughter. He stated that I was on drugs and refused to let him see his daughter. All of this was lies. I was told at the case conference that if I did not give him what he wanted he would go for full custody citing mental health issues. This is exactly what he did. His next affidavit was more lies and ran me into the ground as a mother. I was very shocked that the judge did not rule in his favour, at that time, however, the court case continues. He has refused to settle out of court which I suggested. He has ample money for lawyers whereas I have relied on legal aid.

Please be warned – my emails were accessed and anything I needed for court evidence was deleted. My phone was hacked too and emails deleted from my phone. I have no doubt that my phone calls were listened to. I had three new phones in three years to try to bypass this but was not successful. Please open a new email account and forward everything you need there as well as printing all emails and putting them in a safe place. I recently discovered that files I had stored in the wardrobe of my current house have disappeared too.

I cannot recommend EMDR therapy enough for anyone that has been a victim of abuse. It has been my life-changer and lifesaver. I am a completely different person from the one that escaped the hellhole I was stuck in.

Anglicare is a fabulous resource. Their courses are cheap and counselling is paid on a sliding scale. I attended domestic violence counselling, their ten-week DV course and I began EMDR therapy there.

The Women's Health Organisation in Northbridge, Western Australia, was a great support too. I was given a caseworker and received free counselling which was much needed.

There is a domestic violence unit at Legal Aid which helped me a lot with counselling over the phone.

The government will give a rebate for twenty sessions now, under the mental health care plan. I have seen a psychologist for a number of years now and receive both EMDR as well as counselling therapy.

I am a changed person. I live in peace and happiness. I bear no hatred or bad feelings towards my abuser, that wastes my energy. My life is so much better than it ever was before all of this happened to me.

Realisation

REALISATION.

AS

You are going to be okay!
You are going to be okay. It's the mantra you have to tell yourself. Even on the days you don't think you will be. Even on the days where it's hard to get out of bed and be the highly functioning person you are today. Being a child of domestic abuse is a complicated combination of confusing emotions, which is often impossible to articulate.

The guilt is normal. The guilt that maybe you could have done more. The guilt that maybe you could have broken the toxic cycle that will forever leave permanent scars on your whole family. The guilt that maybe you could have protected your siblings. The guilt that maybe you should have helped your mum. The guilt that you loved your dad. You have to remember, you were only a child. You have to remember you didn't deserve this or do anything wrong.

The 'what-if' is normal. Wondering, *What if this hadn't happened to me?* Wondering, *Why did this have to happen to me?* Fantasising about what life you may have or could have led did you not have to deal with this aspect of your life. Maybe things could have been easier, maybe things could have been better. Maybe they wouldn't have been easier or better, who knows. You have to leave the 'what-ifs' behind, you know it's not healthy. You know

REALISATION.

that you have to tackle what life has delivered. Despite the bad, it has also delivered so much good as well. You have to remind yourself of this on the bad days.

You are going to be okay. Even on those days where you hate being jealous of those around you with loving functional families. Jealous of watching the caring, kind, thoughtful, present fathers around you. Wondering why you drew the short stick of knowing what a physically, emotionally, socially and financially abusive father looks like. Knowing what that feels like. It still gets you down sometimes, and that is okay. That's normal. You need to know life's lows to recognise life's highs.

The shock is normal. The shock of realising you are in a situation that you are not sure how you got into in the first place. The shock of realising that sometimes abuse is so gradual that you don't even realise it's happening until it's gotten so bad. The shock of realising you have suffered trauma. The shock of realising that you have become a victim of a situation you feel powerless against. You are not powerless, in fact, you are stronger than most.

The realisation is normal. As you grow and mature and develop your own friendships and relationships. You form your own family. You realise that none of that was normal. None of those behaviours were acceptable. None of those behaviours were reasonable. None of those behaviours are ones you will ever tolerate again. You've learnt this in the hardest way possible – by watching your loved ones suffer. However, you know, it's made you the strong resilient woman you are today who knows what she does and doesn't want.

You are going to be okay. People think you're hard to crack. Some people even point out that you build up walls and don't let them in. You want to protect yourself from letting people in. You know people have the ability to both love you, but still let you down in every way possible. You are scared of feeling that hurt you know all too well. However, as time goes on you realise that good people can help heal your wounds and look after your scars. They can bring you up, not down. You learn that vulnerability can be beautiful. It is being vulnerable which allows you to have the rich and meaningful relationships you value so greatly in your life.

The anxiety is normal. The anxiety can be triggered by both rational or irrational thoughts. Sometimes it feels crippling, like it's taking over your mind, your body, your life. It's okay to be anxious, it can be a normal human emotion or reaction. You now need to learn the skills to deal with your anxiety and make sure this does not overtake your life. You seek professional help and work through your thoughts, feelings and emotions. You never thought you'd be in a place to confront these demons head-on. The ones you've been suppressing for so long. Thinking that pushing it under the rug was the only way to deal with it all. Most days it felt impossible. There can be light at the end of the tunnel. You know getting control of your anxiety is something well within your power.

The fear is normal. You have nightmares. Unspeakable nightmares of where things could have ended up. Where

> **LIFE HAS SO MANY GOOD THINGS WAITING FOR YOU. SOMETIMES JUST AROUND THE CORNER. YOU CAN'T ALWAYS VISUALISE THEM. BUT IT'S THERE. AND YOU WILL GET THERE. YOU WILL BE OKAY – TRUST ME. OR EVEN BETTER, TRUST YOURSELF. YOU'VE COME THIS FAR ALREADY!**

REALISATION.

things could still end up. For you. For your siblings – your most loyal supporters. For your mum – your biggest cheerleader. You see the occasional headlines. The headlines that most people find unrelatable and unfathomable. For you – these headlines send a dagger through your heart. Make you catch your breath. Make you wipe away a silent tear away. Sometimes you wonder if there will ever be a time where this fear and anxiety will go away. You realise it may never go away and this is something you have to tackle head-on. This is something you are very capable of tackling head-on, you will not let fear or anxiety cripple you. Some days it feels like you're barely hanging on.

You are going to be okay. As you progress through life with these ugly skeletons in your closet. The thoughts, fears and reality you shove under the rug. As you get older, you learn, that actually, everyone has ugly skeletons in their closet. Skeletons in different shapes and different sizes, everyone has them. You are not as alone as you once thought you were. Everyone has their own challenges, big or small. This is what makes us all so wonderfully human. These experiences can be what allows us to feel empathy.

The shame is normal. The misconception that domestic violence only happens in certain families. Lower socioeconomic families. Immigrant families. Indigenous families. But you know that abuse comes in all shapes and sizes. Just like the abusers, and just like the families who are victims of domestic violence. You never know what goes on behind closed doors. People can surprise you. Both for the better or for worse. You never know what it's like to be in someone else's shoes. This teaches you compassion.

The awkwardness is normal. The discomfort when the topic of domestic violence comes up in a setting where you don't feel comfortable talking about it. The situations where you pretend to have no clue what domestic violence truly means. When people share opinions or comments that are completely wrong or ignorant. You want to correct these people. You want to educate them. But sometimes it is not always the time or place, and that is okay. You don't always have to be okay to talk about it.

You are going to be okay. You learn how resilient you are. You also learn where your boundaries are. You learn resilience from your amazing mum. She demonstrates it consistently, despite experiencing unimaginable trauma. You see resilience in your incredible siblings. You know that life throws hurdles – small and large. But your trauma has shaped the woman you are today and made you stronger than you will ever realise. It's set you up to be able to face and overcome life's inevitable challenges.

The happiness is normal too. You learn to celebrate life's wins. You learn to wholeheartedly celebrate both your own and your loved one's wins. The small wins and the big wins. Because you know, better than others, that life isn't always full of wins. And you learn to appreciate the light, because you've seen the dark. Allowing yourself to be happy and celebrate life and your loved ones brings so much joy to your life.

The pride is normal too. You are incredibly proud of all you have achieved, both within your work life and your personal life, despite all the challenges life has thrown at you. Despite all the challenges you continue to face. Despite the poor role modelling you were exposed to. You realise your mum helped overcome that by being a wonderful role model. You are incredibly proud of the good humans that your younger siblings have grown up to be despite the challenges they have faced. They continue to surprise you with their immense maturity and wisdom, often offering you support. You should own all of your achievements, no matter how small or big, as these are all huge in their own right, given the adversity you have had

REALISATION.

to overcome. People may not know this, but you do. And so, you should toot your own horn.

You are going to be okay. You tell yourself this as you notice your father's abusive behaviours start to intensify towards you and your siblings. As he starts to lose control of the women in his life. Those women he called 'his property'. Those women he failed to respect. You wonder if he will ever understand how wrong his abuse was. You wonder if he will ever understand how wrong his abuse still continues to be. You do unfortunately know the disappointing answers to both those questions. It is how you've come to realise that he is no longer someone you want in your life. In fact, he is no longer someone you need or benefit from having in your life.

The doubt is normal. The doubts about the brave things you've done and said to survive and be where you are today. The doubts about the restraining order you've been forced to seek. The doubts about the lawyers you've had to use to protect yourself and your family. The doubts about the police support you've had to seek when he has broken the restraining order. You fight a battle that you're not sure anyone can ever win. But you know it is a battle that you need to fight to protect yourselves, protect your family and send a message that you will not tolerate abuse in any of its forms. Sometimes it feels like the mountain just keeps getting taller.

The anger is normal too. You get angry and frustrated with a system which claims to protect victims, but seems to protect the abusers instead. It's sickening how difficult it is for some women to get help, even when they muster the often impossible courage to try and break out of the abusive cycle. But as time goes on you see more and more charities, advocacy and discussions around domestic violence occur. You start to realise that change is gradually happening, for the better. This is some solace to all of the sadness you've suffered which you wouldn't wish on your worst enemy.

You use this as fuel to speak to others about this issue, to write about this issue and make your own contributions and advocacy.

You are going to be okay. You realise this as you start to deal with the emotions and trauma you have suppressed and compartmentalised for so long. In fact, for your whole life. The time comes when you start to deal with this trauma. You turn to your friends, to professionals, even to podcasts and TV shows. You realise in amazement how strong you are and continue to be having survived so much. You realise how strong so many women and families are having survived these unfortunate situations, and hope that they never forget that.

You are going to be okay. You realise this as life continues on. You realise this as you open up and share your tales and your vulnerabilities with the wonderful people that light up your life. And you realise, as time goes on, these people in your life help ease the burden, heal your soul and help you carry the load.

You are going to be okay. In fact, you are going to be more than okay.

You don't even know when you came to that realisation. It's snuck up on you. You've done some work to get here and it hasn't been easy, but I can tell you that you will be okay.

Life has so many good things waiting for you. Sometimes just around the corner. You can't always visualise them. But it's there. And you will get there. You will be okay – trust me. Or even better, trust yourself. You've come this far already!

injured

INJURED.
Chetna

My husband and I met at my house in India on 3 February 2015. Our parents arranged our meeting for the purpose of marriage. I was twenty-five years old at that time. My father and his father already knew each other. We got engaged on 9 February 2015. We had big ceremony with our family and friends.

My husband and I were married on 15 February 2015 in Jalandhar, Punjab. The ceremony was done according to the Sikh customs. As part of our tradition, the brides give the dowry to the husband's family. We gave gold jewellery, a refrigerator, a TV, a washing machine, a sofa set and a portable air conditioner, as well as a wardrobe, a king-size bed, a sewing machine and cloth for his extended family.

A few weeks after the honeymoon, my in-laws began complaining about the dowry, saying that we had given poor quality items and they were not up to their standards, particularly because their son was NRI – meaning a non-resident Indian. They began demanding cash from my family. I asked them to stop being demanding and they told me that my parents were common people and they were of higher social standing. My husband returned to Perth on 15 March 2015 and I remained with his parents for three months. I had a very hard time during this period. They were very controlling and constantly put restrictions on me. They wanted to dictate what I could wear, where I could go, who I was allowed to speak with. I wasn't even allowed to see my parents by myself, as they insisted on coming with me.

My father-in-law was constantly picking on me, criticising every single thing I did, from how I cooked to how I cleaned. My mother-in-law would often call me names, such as bitch. She also insulted my parents and my sisters, calling them sluts and saying that they sleep around.

On 28 May 2015 I came to Australia on a visitor visa. I stayed for one and a half months. There were no problems at all with my husband during this time. He was very affectionate towards me. My mother-in-law kept calling my husband claiming that she was sick and required me to return to India to help her. On 14 July 2015 I returned to India and went straight to stay with my in-laws. Upon my return, I noticed that there was nothing wrong with my mother-in-law. She seemed perfectly fine. I realised the only reason she needed me back was so she could treat me like her slave again.

I stayed with them for about two months. The treatment I received this time around was even worse than the first time. They continued to be abusive and controlling. One time my father-in-law even hit me with his boots, before my mother-in-law intervened and said that he should not hit me, because I may tell my parents and then they may get into trouble.

My in-laws was constantly reporting back to my husband saying that I was lazy, that all I did was sleep and stay in my room and that I was not helping her at all. None of this was true.

On 18 September 2015 I travelled to Perth again on a visitor visa. This time I noticed an immediate change in my husband. It was obvious that he was upset with me over the allegations his parents had made.

Between September 2015 and March 2016, when I was in Perth

on a visitor visa, my relationship with my husband was okay. But he would often prohibit me from going anywhere while he was at work. He would also dictate what I should eat. For example, I was not allowed to eat anything with eggs, as he did not like eggs. I was not allowed to eat any type of meat, as he was a vegetarian and insisted that I become a vegetarian also.

While in India with my husband, we got into an argument about my side of the family. His parents and my husband made fun of my sisters, saying that they dressed badly and un-Indian. They also made fun of my father saying that he was stupid. I defended my family but they carried on. I told my husband that he should stop doing this. He then kicked me with his feet while I was sitting on the bed. I then fell off the bed and he hit my head against the window behind me. My husband and his parents then laughed at me while I was on the ground.

My partner visa was granted in March 2016 and I returned to Perth with my husband on 18 April 2016. When I moved to Australia on my partner visa, I began looking for work, but was unsuccessful. One evening I discussed the work issue with my husband. He was getting angry and frustrated with me for not being able to find work. I told him not to push me and pointed out that his mother never worked a day in her life, so why was he getting angry with me for not finding work. He then slapped me really hard in the face. My face became swollen and my jaw was aching. I struggled to eat for two or three days.

In September 2016, my father-in-law called my husband complaining that I had put a photo of myself on my WhatsApp profile. He said that now I was a married woman, if I was to be put up a photo at all, it should be with my husband. My husband then confronted me about this. I told my husband that his father had no right to interfere and tell me what photo I was allowed to use on my own profile. My husband then began abusing me verbally, screaming and calling me names, like slut and bitch. He then threatened to sabotage my family's reputation and threatened to kill me and send my dead body to my parents in India.

In October 2016 my husband and I were arguing about something, I don't remember what the topic was. He then became angry and threw a plate at me. The plate hit my chin. I began crying hysterically and my husband became even more enraged. He then grabbed the pot of rice I had cooked and dumped it in the bin. He then told me to eat it. My chin was bruised the next day. After this incident things were mainly okay with my husband for a few months with no major incident.

In May 2017, my in-laws came to visit from India. I always dreaded it when they said they would visit. They had been so cruel and abusive in the past. So I knew that this time would be no different. As soon as they arrived, my mother-in-law began nagging about the dowry again; saying that it was inadequate and we should give them more. My mother-in-law would also always encourage me to stop speaking with my parents in an attempt to make me estranged from them, I believe that she wanted this so that she could control me even more and prevent me from telling my parents what they were doing to me. My mother-in-law constantly shouted at me, saying that she would make sure that my life was ruined. She would also tell me that she would kick me out of the house. When I spoke to my husband about this he told me that there was nothing that he could do because his mother owned the house and that she could do as she pleased.

On 1 June 2017 an argument ensued and my husband slapped me on my face two or three times. His mother soon joined in and began hitting my shoulders. I told her to stop. My husband then held my hands behind my back and his mother then slapped me on my face two or three more times. After that my husband picked up his phone and called my father. He went to the garage but I could hear him shouting. He told my father that he would kill me and send my body to India. After that I grabbed my phone and purse and ran to my neighbour Gurpreet's house. I asked her to call the domestic violence helpline for me. While I was on the phone with them, my husband came to Gurpreet's house, and began to shout at her. Gurpreet told him to stop shouting or she would call the police. After a few hours things calmed down and I returned home.

> **I WANT WOMEN TO SPEAK OUT ABOUT WHAT IS HAPPENING TO THEM. I WANT TO STIR SOCIETY INTO ACTION. WOMEN ARE NOT MADE TO BE USED OR TORTURED.**

My in-laws left in August 2017. During their entire visit, they repeatedly nagged me about the dowry, told me that my family was poor, ridiculing my family and degrading me. My husband continued to be abusive to me in all ways possible.

In December 2017, I found out that I was pregnant. I told my husband about this and he was shocked. He ultimately told me that I must choose between the baby and our marriage. He was deadset on me to having an abortion. I pleaded with him to keep the baby but he was not interested. He was like a mad man. He took me to a medical centre, who then referred me to an abortion clinic in Midland. I attended the clinic with him, doctors gave me tablets for an abortion. My husband made me open my mouth to make sure that I had taken them. I began to bleed and I was in alot of pain. The next day I returned to clinic and I had a surgical abortion.

At the end of December I travelled to India to attend my sister's wedding. My husband did not come with me. I returned to Perth after receiving a letter from the Department of Home Affairs in January 2018 that my husband had withdrawn his sponsorship and broken the relationship. After an argument in February he kicked me out of the house and I have been living at a women's refuge since February 2018. Since moving to refuge I have been receiving a lot of counselling and have learned to respect myself. We got divorced in 2019.

I feel that my marriage with him had alot of ups and downs. We had some good times where he was affectionate towards me. Then there was also so many times where he had been disrespectful, demeaning and abusive to me. Despite all that, I tried my absolute best to make my marriage work as I had genuinely grown to love my husband and I wanted to the best wife possible for him. But he was listening to his mother as always who never liked me. That's why he decided to end this marriage.

Then last year, in 2020, I saw my ex-husband's photo in the newspaper with the rape charges on him. He assaulted a teenage girl at his workplace. He has been proven guilty and jailed. I was feeling sorry for that teenage girl but at the same time I felt justice was given.

As a woman from India I was not aware of my rights and my self-respect. When I came to women's refuge, I realised how much I suffered during this abusive relationship. I am thinking, *Why did I stay in that relationship for three years?* I would like to advise all women that if you feel the same, please be strong to move out from an abusive relationship. I will always regret not doing that sooner. I was not that confident and over time I have become aware that I have been through a lot.

Unappreciated

UNAPPRECIATED.
Chris

Never mind the darkness, we can still find a way – those are the words I keep telling myself over and over again about myself and my sons.

My name is Chris. I am a mother of two boys. My story starts like every other couple we meet. When I was twenty-two years old we fell in love, when I was twenty-four I fell pregnant and gave birth to a baby boy. Not long after, when he was a few months old, we moved in together.

Everything seemed fine for some years but slowly he started to alienate me from my friends and family. I realised I was all alone and relying on him more and more. Six years later my second son was born.

There were many years of verbal abuse, controlling ways, bad tempers and occasional physical abuse such as slaps to the head, pushes in the back – just enough not to leave any physical signs on my body. I sought help through a crisis centre, my children and I were put up in a hotel, helped to secure Centrelink payments, but after five days I was told I could no longer stay at the hotel and needed to find other accommodation. With no extra income and no references, I had nowhere to go so we ended up back home with him.

After a few more years, and saving as much as I could, I found the courage to leave, I secured a rental property and was days away from leaving. But before my children and I got to leave we found him unconscious and in an incoherent state early one morning. After being rushed to the hospital he was diagnosed with a brain tumour.

Despite all my courage and effort in gaining strength to leave he managed to make me feel so sorry for him that I stayed.

I thought he would change after his near-death experience, I was hopeful and prayed things would be different. How wrong I was. As his illness and treatment progressed, so did his verbal abuse with constant remarks like, 'You stupid mole, pathetic excuse for a human being. You are fat no wonder I can't get turned on, no man would ever want to fuck you, you should be grateful I do. You're so fucked up in the head you need help, your slit [which refers to my vagina] is so big it's no wonder I don't enjoy rooting you.'

At times the verbal abuse got so vulgar and disgusting I wondered how I was going to get through it all. I can't recall how many times he has called me a slag, whore, fucked up bitch that smells like a fish factory, a wasted space in this world – among many other names.

As his illness got more intense, I had to give up work. Because of the tumour, he was having seizures regularly which meant he was unable to drive so I was the one taking him to his hospital appointments, which were often several times a week. He would also call my work saying he was having a seizure or he needed help so I would have to come home, but most of the time it was to just get me home.

Every time I got stronger emotionally and tried to leave or even mentioned leaving, he would threaten to hurt my horse and my dogs, say that he would find me and make me pay, and I might even know what it was like to lose a child.

No matter what I did, nothing was ever good enough, I tried to give in to having sex or performing oral sex many times a week in the hope it would keep him happy but unfortunately, he always wanted it more. Making me feel guilty by saying his balls hurt from the build-up of sperm and just going on and on relentlessly about how I don't know what it is like to be a man and not release your sacks, until I gave in – *Why?* you ask – because giving in gave me peace for a little while, otherwise he would go on for hours and not even let me sleep.

As my children grew up it was becoming harder to keep things from them, they realised he had a temper and was starting to try and control them. No matter the conversation or topic of discussion, he was always right. He would tell them something then say he didn't say that and started having them question what was said. This, I found out, is called gaslighting, which I have experienced so many times I started questioning my own memory and apologising so much I felt there might have been something wrong with me. It took me a very long time to realise it was his way to control situations and make me doubt myself so much that I relied on him more and more.

He would always try to reinforce gender roles by saying it is my responsibility to clean, cook, look after him and the children – he didn't even do much parenting with his boys. I was the one who attended their sporting commitments, helped them with homework, encouraged them to strive for what they wanted.

My youngest son was a good little soccer player. He played soccer in primary school for seven years – not once did his father attend any games and when my son tried to tell his dad about them, the response he got was, 'Only dogs chase balls.' My son stopped trying to talk to his dad about his love of playing soccer after that.

Move forward a few years, his cancer went into remission, he got his licence back – this gave me a bit more freedom, and as I owned a horse, I got to ride and spend more time riding and volunteering at my horse club. Rather than being happy for me, the accusations started about how much time I was spending with my horse and volunteering at my club. He said that volunteering is for suckers and that I was being used by everyone and that I was weak because I couldn't see that they were using me. He would go on and on about it so much to the extent of making me feel guilty about enjoying my time with my horse and volunteering that it was easier to just spend as little time as possible helping and riding.

I was always walking on eggshells, feeling like nothing I did was ever good enough or I wasn't even good enough. I was even questioning my parenting skills because he was always telling me I was a stupid, pathetic excuse for a mother, and that when my children grew up, they would walk all over me because I had no control over them because I was weak and showed no discipline.

By now I had learnt a lot more about domestic violence and tried to get out a few times, but each time he manipulated me and made threats against me. So to protect myself and my children I always went back.

For a long while I never told too many people about what was happening – people judge and often blame the victim and think they are trying to cause trouble. Unless you have experienced DV you would not understand the sacrifices we go through to protect ourselves, our children, family and even our pets.

Many times, I have been asked, 'Why don't you just leave? How hard is it to just walk out?'

Well, when he sees that a woman has been killed by her ex-partner his response was, 'Well she probably deserved it.' And when I say if two people don't love each other anymore and feel they need to separate then they should be able to, his response is, 'Like hell – if you ever leave you would be so sorry. That's if you live long enough.'

Twelve years after his brain tumour diagnosis (doctors did not expect him to live past five years) his tumour came back. He had another operation to remove it but he didn't come out of it too well and he lost some mobility in his left leg and arm.

I was now his full-time carer and the dynamics in our relationship were changing. He was relying on me for a lot of his daily care needs. His gaslighting ways were becoming more and more as he tried to make me doubt my sanity, judgment and memories.

He started to blame me for not having any illness or mobility issues by saying I should be the one that was sick as he had the right to live longer than me because I did nothing to contribute to society whereas he's been a great asset to the world.

He told me constantly that I should be having sex with him as much as possible because when he's not here anymore I won't ever get it again as no man would want me, as I am frigid and useless at sex anyway.

He harassed our youngest son, who is twenty now, telling him he was lazy, stupid and he wouldn't ever amount to anything but a compulsive liar and selfish person. My son has a good job, works hard and is a very intelligent person.

There was an altercation, one of a few, where his father lashed out and grabbed him around the neck and started to strangle him. My eldest son and I were pulling him off when he turned and grabbed me and threw me so hard against the cupboard it knocked the wind out of me. My youngest then grabbed his father and smacked him in the mouth causing him to fall. He said to him if he ever touched his mum again he would be sorry.

Now my partner had realised he had lost his control over his son – he kicked him out, telling him never to return home again and as far as he was concerned, he wasn't his son anymore.

As a mum this broke my heart, I felt I had let my son down and

I could no longer protect him, so encouraging him to stay would only make his life miserable. So, I did what I had to do and gave him money, helped him every day where I could and let him know I was there for him no matter what.

As a mum I have done an amazing job of raising my two sons. My youngest, despite being forced out of the family home, has managed to buy himself a home and be free of his fathers' control and violence. Our relationship as mother and son is still as strong as ever and I will continue to be his mother and help him when or if he ever needs it.

Jump ahead to 2021, fourteen years after being first diagnosed with his brain tumour – things are going downhill for him, he has lost almost all mobility in his left leg and is now confined to a wheelchair permanently, and with limited movement in his left arm, he is now dependent on me for almost all daily tasks.

It is very hard for him to physically abuse me anymore but his verbal abuse has gotten so much worse as have his threats of having me hurt or incapacitated so I can feel what it is like being a disabled person like him.

Even though he relies totally on me for everything, it has not stopped his coercive control with constant threats, humiliation, intimidation, blaming me for everything – even his illness – creating drama and trying to make me feel guilty as I am not sick and he is. I endure this abuse on a daily basis over and over again.

With his tumour continuing to grow despite chemotherapy and radiation therapy, his life expectancy is decreasing, and one day in the near future it will take his life, so until then I need to keep my spirits up and my wits about me and continue to survive this nightmare.

Nearly every discussion we have is somehow twisted to where I am to blame for something that occurred. Even when I try to discuss how his behaviour makes me feel, he can twist the conversation and end up blaming me. Saying things like, 'You need help, you are a psychotic, nasty twisted person who cares for no-one but yourself and does nothing for me.'

When he is in the wrong, he denies it. He won't take responsibility, changes it so it was my fault he was wrong because I am trying to make him look bad or confuse him to try and take advantage of him because he is sick. Everything is about him even when I am sick myself or run-down – it is always how lazy I am and I do not know what being sick is, I am just weak and pathetic.

Some days I am scared to eat, as he sees me eating a sandwich or piece of cheese, then the verbal attacks start by saying how fat I am, how flabby my body is – he says he doesn't know why I even go to the gym it's not working, actually, it is making me fatter.

I was always second-guessing myself, wondering, *Is it just me,* I was finding it hard to make decisions, he has made me feel inadequate as a person, lonely and insecure – until palliative care stepped in due to his illness. With palliative care came a social worker, and although he is a male, he got my trust and I opened up to him, telling him things that I had hidden deep inside.

Through his counselling and through my own determination and strong will, I have found the courage and strength to hang in there because cancer will take his life, and my children and I will be free and I will be able to use my resources, knowledge and experiences to help other victims and survivors of DV.

Sex is non-existent anymore due to his illness which is a godsend for me, even though he continues to blame me for his impotency and still tries to coerce me into having sex. But I am remaining strong and will continue to do what I have to, to stay safe and plan for my future.

Leaving at this stage is very dangerous so by staying it ensures the safety of myself and my sons, so I am hanging in there. Some days are so hard and unbearable – the verbal abuse is relentless, vulgar and nasty. I have heard it many times over and over again how I am a fucking useless mole, can't drive, pathetic bitch who is selfish, doesn't deserve to live, as well as he thinks I should be the one dying of cancer, not him, as I deserve to be suffering as I have made his life so miserable.

His unpredictable behaviour, the sick fantasies he conjures up, relentless belittling and threats are becoming more and more frequent as he realises they do not have the impact he wants on me as I am getting stronger and more resilient.

I am just seeing the light at the end of the tunnel as the cancer is getting worse – one day in the near future we will be free and we can enjoy a nice peaceful life.

My horses have been my solace in helping me get through this for many years, as well as keeping me focused on surviving every nightmare I have endured as well as giving me confidence and a state of control over my life.

> **LIVING IN A DV SITUATION IS HARD ENOUGH. DO WHATEVER IT TAKES TO BE SAFE AND KEEP FOCUSED. FIND SOMETHING YOU CAN FIND PEACE WITH AND CONCENTRATE ON THAT UNTIL YOU FIND THE COURAGE TO ESCAPE BUT DO IT WITH SUPPORT AND PLAN EVERY ASPECT OF THE MOVE.**

Resilient

RESILIENT.
Ronnie

'You are used goods. No-one will want you. You're damaged property. Who do you think will ever take on a woman with a kid? Where are you gonna go? Back to your mother's? Live with your sister?' These were the constant reminders during arguments. Giving me little hope of a chance to ever leave. The words that forever haunted me and that I took for gospel holding me back from leaving the toxic relationship.

I was born in South Africa and arrived in Australia when I was four years old, along with my parents and older sister. We grew up middle class and had attended public schools. Family was number one. Weekends were spent together and often with South African friends. My mother did shiftwork as a nurse at Royal Perth Hospital while my father was a boilermaker by trade, working Monday to Friday. My sister had a goal and future-focused mindset by setting up her financial future. My father had instilled in her that education was key. I don't remember him telling me that. Following in the footsteps of an intelligent sister often resulted in disappointment as I continuously had self-doubt in my abilities. When I did apply myself, I did succeed. I didn't take school seriously and missed the opportunity to learn. It was more of a social scene. I was a rebellious teenager. Skipped school, caught with drugs and schoolyard fights. I was allowed to attend parties and didn't have responsibilities and chores like my sister did at the same age. This caused tension in our relationship, and then she became more like a mother figure, scalding me when I got in trouble. However, as we moved into adulthood, we became a lot closer along with our friendship groups moulding.

As a twenty-year-old, life was played out day by day. Clubbing and socialising. So, when I met him, I never expected a possible lifelong relationship. We had previously met through friends at a nightclub. But he didn't seem to recall that moment. I was in a three-year relationship with James, which had abruptly ended when I had found out he was cheating on me for months. It was a Wednesday in February of 2008. I was devasted, heartbroken and in pieces. A friend, Anne, wanted to take my mind off my recent break-up with James and invited me out to drink and dance at the Leederville Hotel. It was there that I reconnected with him. I told him who James had just been caught with and how I feared for my safety, due to this new girl's family and reputation. I recall us exchanging numbers, hiding our Nokias, under the table like schoolkids. He said, 'Don't worry, I'll protect you.'

The honeymoon phase always puts your perspective into a haze, like you're looking at the world through rose-coloured glasses. The beginning was memorable. The conversations on the landline that went on for hours, waking up with each other on our minds and not being able to wait to see each other – it seemed like a dream. What I look back on now, is how our relationship was officiated, he said, 'You know you're mine now? You're my girlfriend.' Within the first few weeks, he invited me down south to join him on a working trip to Busselton and Bunbury. He told me how nervous he was even asking. A month later, he messed up the dates on which his parents returned from their holiday, and we had a spontaneous meeting. I had met his brothers already.

His family lived out in the Swan Valley, on acreage, with beautiful, scenic sunset views. I felt like Cinderella. I had never been accustomed to what I believed was such wealth before. His father is Italian with a construction company and his mother is Australian, who was at the time, a stay-at-home mum. He was the eldest of four boys. I was, indeed, made to feel like a princess, being the only girl in the family. His mother and I spoke fashion and often shared our latest buys. His father and I enjoyed a wine or two, overlooking the beautiful landscape. I'd regularly banter with his brothers and gang up teasing him.

> **NEVER LET THE FEAR OF STRIKING OUT KEEP YOU FROM PLAYING THE GAME.**
> **– BABE RUTH**

He, however, favoured his Italian heritage with whom he'd formed friendships with through family connections and associating with rough people. They enjoyed riding their quad bikes and Harley-Davidsons along with trips out to the farm and shooting targets. That side to him didn't impress me as it would certain other girls. It did, however, become beneficial when we were clubbing and attending festivals. I felt cool. Like I was a part of the 'in-crowd'. People knew who we were. A popular couple in our younger days and I knew I was untouchable. We partied almost every weekend, and I would sleep over his house more than often. I had obtained my licence a bit later than usual. So, before I had completed the test, he was regularly picking me up and detouring to drop me off before he went to work.

He was initially a carpenter, by trade. With connections through his family and working relationships, he soon began his period working FIFO (FIFO stands for fly-in fly-out. This means that workers are brought to site for the length of their work roster and are provided with accommodation, recreation facilities, meals, etc.). During this time, he was able to save the money he was making, rather than spend it every RnR (rest and recuperation) like most men. He obtained his (our) first investment property, which was soon leased and out of our worries. Soon after, he purchased and leased out our first home. By this time, I had moved into his parent's house, which had plenty of space, however, we were confined to one room. On his time off, he had managed to build a granny flat created from a demountable classroom, in which he created our first little house.

As our relationship grew, along came the arguments. Although, initially, he wasn't as controlling. He made it difficult and uncomfortable when I wanted to socialise with my friends. We lived forty-five minutes east of the city. If I were to have a big night out with the girls, I would need to sleep out or not drink as taxis home would cost too much. I soon became distant with my friends as when I would ask if I could go out, he would make me feel horrible and say, 'What am I supposed to do with myself now? What am I meant to have for dinner?' In the end, I just stopped asking and going out. I was always welcome with his friends when the girls were around. But he was embarrassing around my friends, with the inappropriate comments he'd often make. When we did have arguments, before going out to family events, he would act like nothing had happened and play the victim once we were out. I look back at the narcissistic behaviour, allowing me to think I'm crazy when I was acting like a so-called bitch afterwards.

I remember organising a night out with my best friend Jessica. I ensured I let him know well in advance and suggested he have a boys' night. Then the night arrived and I began getting ready. When he had come home from work, he was furious when realising that I was going out. There was yelling and name-calling.

He smashed my phone against the wall, completely breaking the screen when I was trying to message Jessica. I recall him grabbing my arms and shaking me while he was yelling, until he had his hand on my throat then my mouth to keep me from screaming – in case his parents heard in the main house. As I tried to run out of our bedroom and to the front door, he barricaded me in. That was the first time he hit me. That evening he continued to watch movies and Foxtel and fell asleep on the couch in the bedroom, like nothing had happened. I was lucky enough to have my iPad that was connected to my phone which was the only way to really message Jessica to say I wasn't going to come out.

We went through the cycle of violence. Once he was violent, he then went through the apologetic stage then back to a normal relationship and back into a honeymoon phase and then the arguments would arise again. Through multiple fights, I rarely had the physical bruises to prove it. Otherwise punches to the walls and doors were prevalent. I had run over to his parents' house crying but, in the end, it felt like a counselling session and that they didn't believe me.

As the years went by the relationship was average. His family were so generous. We'd often travel to Bali where absolutely everything was paid for. They were such a close family unit and I felt welcomed. They had family dogs, along with ours, so I took on the responsibility of taking care of them. He was rough with our dog, who often cowered when he was near, fearful of being hurt.

In July 2012, I had just returned from a European holiday with a couple of my girlfriends. After returning to work I remember coming home one evening and finding the house was completely spotless. There was a bouquet of flowers on the table and music playing. To my surprise, he proposed that day. I don't remember what he said as I was quite emotional but I said yes. I ran outside and I saw his parents were waiting to congratulate us. Our wedding was in 2014 at Caversham House. No expense was spared. I had organised most of the wedding by myself in-between working full-time. I organised detailed proceedings for the day, however by the time the wedding had arrived the day just felt like a party for him. I spent most of night looking for him because he spent most of the evening outside with his friends. He passed out on the ride back home. His family paid for and accompanied us during our honeymoon. I didn't mind and preferred having their company over his.

Soon after we were married, we moved into one of our investment properties in Midland, Western Australia. This was a house ready for renovations. I had been working at Myer, so my money was essentially for decorating the house and ensuring the fridge and pantry were full of everything that he required. In the evenings I needed to make sure that dinner was ready, whether he was eating it or not.

After a few years of trying, I finally fell pregnant. I remember crying, but not with tears of joy. This was both a happy and fearful moment. Although he paid for the nursery furniture, he failed to build it, leaving me to do so while six months pregnant, along with organising the entire room. He did, however, attend all the pregnancy classes and scans. I ended up at forty weeks and five days, before I was induced. Starting on a Friday afternoon, and through the various methods, I was unsuccessful in dilation. Our son was born Monday afternoon via an emergency C-section, where I was only allowed to see him for a moment before he was whisked away. The first day I was bedridden and unable to see, touch or hold my son. Arriving home, my husband was not helpful. He slept eight hours every night in the spare bedroom and left me with the baby in the master bedroom. Both tired and depressed, I hadn't formed a bond with the baby. After a few weeks he finally did take the baby, from the early hours in the morning allow me a few hours rest.

During an intense argument, when my son was one month old, I had to stay overnight with his parents. With little hope of any reassurance, I returned to play the good wife again.

It was the first week of December. My son was only eight weeks old by this time, and my husband needed to return to work at a construction business that he had formed and built up. As the morning hours went by, I just wanted him out of the house, to leave me in peace. My constant 'nagging' triggered him. I would ask him when he was leaving and why he was lying on the couch watching TV. I remember him yelling at me to STFU. I wasn't one to keep quiet. While I was holding my son, he slapped me so hard across my face, my cheek tingled for hours. After resting my son on his playmat, he cornered me in the kitchen and choked me. Once I was free, I had no choice but to leave. I left my son on the playmat and jumped in my car and left. He assumed I'd return, as I usually did. I felt I couldn't go to his or my parents, nor the police, in case they didn't believe me. I found myself driving to the local child health nurse office, to a nurse who assisted during check-ups. I was shattered and beyond words. She contacted the police and after many calls, organised a safe house for me. The police accompanied me back to the house, and my husband was arrested, allowing me to pack a suitcase of whatever I could find, and take our son.

I arrived at the women's refuge exhausted. After the formalities, I was shown to our unit. I was forever grateful, walking into a house with a pantry and fridge full of food. Full toiletries and baby care were all provided, with a cot and bouncer. The first few weeks were stressful as I had begun to engage with my lawyer and organise a Violence Restraining Order. He immediately sought legal advice and had documents filed to restrict our son from leaving the state. He thought I'd run away. Before I could have my initial consultation with my lawyer, he had contacted and planned with a mediator. As I was not able to attend, he was instantly awarded the certificate, allowing court proceedings to occur. I stayed there for eight weeks, over Christmas and New Year's, until I was able to have my government parenting entitlements and legal documents sorted. I moved back in with my parents, taking the master bedroom. This time, I allowed my mother to assist with caring for my son. It was during this time, I began attending group therapy sessions for domestic violence survivors. Situated next to the child health nurses' office I had originally fled to, with each term, I built up my self-confidence. I was also attending one on one sessions. Along with some of the beauties I had met in those group sessions, that year I attended my first White Ribbon silent walk event.

With little education, I decided to begin my university journey. In September 2018, I enrolled in the Graduate Certificate in Business at the University of Western Australia. During my first month, I took advantage of attending a first Friday networking event led by the MBA student social club committee. It was during these events, and attending the end of year ball, that allowed me to meet a diverse range of different students. The following year, I joined the committee. Completing the necessary core units, and maintaining the set average, I graduated allowing me to continue studying the full Master's Degree in Business. At this time, I was able to regularly attend functional fitness classes, at a F45, that my friend Jessica managed. This allowed me to set personal fitness goals to shed the baby weight.

By June of 2019, I was able to move into my sister's two by one rental. I was so grateful to finally have our own space along with my son's very own room. With assistance from my family and by saving my parenting payments, I was able to furnish my house with all second-hand goods.

While juggling studies and a young child, I returned to Myer as a part-time employee. I gradually lost job satisfaction with a team of managers who were all undervalued. With the support of family and friends, I was able to confidently attend court appearances, which ended up being family consultant meetings. It was here that we needed to negotiate parenting and financial orders. I'm thankful for the lawyer, which I referred to as a 'bulldog'. She took no nonsense and I felt well represented. I'm grateful my mother was able to fund the thirty-thousand-dollar-plus bill. By this time, I didn't renew the restraining order as having parents conduct handovers became unsuitable and inconvenient. I understood that he wouldn't risk harming me for the sake of potentially losing the rights with his son. He continued to run the once-multi-million-dollar business into the ground, as the books say. With the low-income declaration, I ended up receiving scraps compared to what I should have been, I couldn't prove the 'cashies' he would be doing, as he always has. He organised buyers for the properties which left us with barely anything to split.

As the COVID-19 pandemic swept the globe, I had growing concerns regarding future employment in retail. In March 2021, I had organised a dinner with a mutual friend through uni, and one of our lockdown restrictions were due to end that evening. At the end of the night, she starts to talk about the perfect position that had become available with her business. Soon after, my interview was conducted and I was offered the position. Working as an operations consultant, within the resources sector, I was out of my comfort zone. With the flexibility for day care drop-offs and the ability of working remote, I have found the perfect role with the opportunity to progress while completing the last units of my degree. Through Instagram, I found the perfect personal trainer. Her business is based around WHY. Together, we have set fitness goals leading into next year, where I intend to compete in fitness model shows.

As I look over the past four years, I have learnt more about myself and grown in confidence. I was always a strong and independent woman. But during the ten-year relationship, I lost who I was. By next year, with the assistance of my mortgage broker, I aim to buy a house with a backyard for my son. My personal, fitness and career development plans are in motion. Every decision I make is for my son and for our future. I will always put us first.

UNHEALED

UNHEALED.
Anonymous

Looking back at it all now, you could say that my life was destined to never be smooth sailing. When my mother was pregnant with me she attempted to abort me many times, but the procedure always failed. I guess it was distilled in me that I was always going to be a fighter. I grew up in Thailand with my mum, my dad and seven other siblings. My dad was good-looking and was always having affairs. He was known to be a playboy and even had the nerve to call one of my sister's by his mistress' name!! He would always be fighting with my mum. My mum never left, she sacrificed her happiness and stayed with him. She soldiered on and looked after all of us. My mum was a very loving, devoted mother, but at the same time, she was very controlling, and in our culture, we always respected our elders, especially our parents.

I respected my mum so much that when she made me choose between my son (who I had at age seventeen) and her, I of course chose her. She was very strict, at times she would beat me and rub salt on my wounds. She forced me to marry someone I wasn't even in love with. He treated me like absolute crap. He would smoke and drink for days on end and did not give a shit about me.

I needed to get away, so I took a bus from Thailand to Singapore, where my brother was working. My sister-in-law and I went out and partied, and that's where I met Tim.

I really wanted a better life for myself, so he sponsored me to be a citizen. I told my mum I was moving away so that I could work and make money.

I then migrated to Australia in 1980. Tim worked hard and provided for me. We were happy and welcomed our daughter into this world together. I honestly thought I had struck gold and my life was turning in a good direction. That was before I found out that he had an affair with his best friend's young girlfriend.

I was so heartbroken that I wanted to dance my sorrows away so I went to a nightclub – not expecting to meet the love of my life. He was younger than me and studying in Perth.

We got together and I ended up falling pregnant, but at eight months pregnant, due to have a girl, he decided to leave me for another woman. He did come back into my life when she was eleven months old. My heart was still his, and we went on to have another daughter. Of course, my luck with men was cursed – it ended and we went our separate ways.

I was left heartbroken yet again. One of my best friends saw I was depressed, so she took me to a nightclub. That night she introduced me to John, so that I could move on and forget about my ex. Gosh, I remember him so clearly! He was so handsome, funny, talked so sweetly to me and bought me drinks throughout the night. He was a true gentleman – he swept me off my feet. After that night we contacted each other and spoke every day, and after one month we became a couple. At this time, I already had three daughters but he didn't mind and accepted that they were in my sole care.

I was a single mum, who cared for my girls on my own. I was able to receive government payments to survive. At that time, I lived in an old, tiny flat with my girls. John and I thought it would be a good idea for him to live in the same block but separately.

It was about three months into our relationship, when the honeymoon stage was fading, that his true colours started coming out. The arguing began and that's when the abuse started. There are many times I remember so clearly. One time we were arguing, and out of nowhere, he punched me right in my stomach. You'd think that, in itself, was a warning sign to leave. But I didn't. I had hope that it would get better, and I would blame myself for always talking back to him, so I deserved it. Another time, my kids were sleeping and we started arguing, he punched me in the face, sat on my stomach and repeatedly hit me. He literally beat the shit out of me. I had shat myself!!

Another clear memory was one morning I was busy plaiting my daughter's hair for school. John asked me to make him eggs for breakfast, I said no, I was busy getting the girls ready. He did not like or accept that answer. He was not happy that I didn't put him first. He grabbed my hair and dragged me to the kitchen to boil eggs, all whilst my three children were there watching in fear. I never dared to fight back as I was so scared that he would hurt me even more – or hurt my girls. He would always slap me around and pull my hair out, leaving bald patches.

We had this huge fight and I had finally had enough, so I went to the police to report him. The police advised me not to go back to the house, so they arranged for my girls and me to stay at a women's refuge.

Immediately I saw happiness in their eyes. People were so lovely and caring – it was a breath of fresh air. I was so torn that I had put my children through this suffering. My poor kids always had to witness his outbursts, our arguing, him beating me up. We stayed there for about a month until I got approved for a government house. It was heartbreaking letting the girls know we were no longer were staying there. They cried and asked if they could stay, because they were afraid of John. Unfortunately, our time was up, and we needed to move into our new home.

We settled in nicely, and then *SURPRISE,* he was back in the picture. He promised me that things would change. I fell pregnant – you guessed, it another girl. The abuse kept happening, we were on and off ALL THE TIME. I had this feeling that he was seeing someone else. So, I went to his house and looked through the window, and standing there, right before my eyes, he was with a girl, giggling and laughing. I stood there with tears running down my face. Absolutely numb. Stupidly, I accepted him back and we continued the relationship. Everything with him made me so stressed out that I went into false labour at six months pregnant. I was admitted to King Edward Memorial Hospital, and thankfully she did not come out that early.

You'd honestly think that the violence would stop, given how much stress he put me through. It got so bad that I had to waddle my way, with my three girls, to court to get a restraining order against him. However, the sweet-talker worked his magic and I eventually had it revoked.

We welcomed our first child together. I was so in love and thought that things truly could get better. Nope, I was wrong! He punched me in front of my sister, and she yelled at him to stop. He then turned to her and showed his fist and said, 'Do you want some?' She was so frightened she ran away. She begged me to leave him and said that she would take care of the girls and me. But I was too scared to leave. I now had a child with him. My friends and family knew about the abuse, but no-one

> **ONCE IT STARTS, IT DOESN'T STOP. LEAVE THE FIRST TIME HE HITS YOU, PLEASE.**

dared to do or say anything because they were all so scared for their lives and mine.

He somehow swept me off my feet again, just like how he did when we met. I fell pregnant once more.

Seven months into the pregnancy, I was feeling huge and exhausted. He wanted to have sex and I said no. As you could imagine, everything always had to be his way. No was not an answer for him. He raped me. Tears flowing uncontrollably, my stomach cramping up, my heart shattering into pieces. I was left there feeling so uncomfortable and violated.

Shortly after, I gave birth to a boy, and all my heartache and pain went away. Life surely would have to get better, right? WRONG. The hair-pulling, the slapping, the punching, the name-calling, kept going on and on.

One day I was out visiting my family, so I left him a plate of food. I wasn't home to warm it up for him so he got so angry. When I arrived at home he threw the plate at me, like it was a frisbee, and it cut open my skin close to my temple. My face felt wet and I thought it was just the food from the plate. I looked at my son and his face was pale. I went to the bathroom and realised why. I was drenched in blood, I cried so hard and so much that I could see the white from my bones. My youngest daughter cried and begged to call 000. He pretended like he didn't know what she was on about and brushed it off. After a few hours of me begging him to take me, he eventually took me to the hospital, where I got stitched up. They said lucky it didn't hit my temple, otherwise I would have been dead. The doctors were aware of the abuse, so they wanted to keep me overnight. He questioned why the hell would they need me to stay overnight, just for stitches?! I acted dumb and said I didn't know. *Ahhhh* ... Finally, my one night of not being abused.

Back to reality ... Honestly, when was I ever going to catch a break? Years passed, and I had to go to the doctor because I felt lumps in my breast. They turned out to be cysts from all the stress I was going through. Whilst I was in the waiting room, a conversation started with a kind lady. We chatted about life and our backgrounds. I felt safe enough to open up about the abuse going on in my life. She was a lady from a Christian church – Potter's House. She told me to come along, and that is where I found my faith in God. Shortly after, I became a born-again Christian. I stayed in that church for many years until my daughter became best friends with a girl whose dad was a pastor. We would go to their house every Wednesday and Sunday for fellowship. On other days he would come over to say a prayer. I would always pray and ask for forgiveness – I'd be crying and holding my Bible and praying so hard for there to be a light at the end of the tunnel. I asked God to make a way for my life to be better. Finally – and thank God – the burden lifted, and my prayers were answered. John found another woman, he was able to leave me alone.

After a while, I managed to find my confidence again. I was introduced to Barry, and there was something different about him. He was kind-hearted, caring and loved all my kids unconditionally. Life was looking like it was going to give me a breather, for once. Until one day, John called me and asked if I did homework with Lara. I said I hadn't, but Barry was reading with her. John demanded that Lara get on the phone and read to him. As she sounded out the words, he did not like the fact that she was taking 'too long'. He drove over to our house and knocked on the flyscreen as if there was no tomorrow. It's slightly a blur as to how he got into the house, but then he started going off at me. Barry stepped in and tried to diffuse the situation. John turned to him and said, 'It's none of your business!!'

Barry replied, 'Yes it is, because you're in the house that I pay for and I'm the one reading with your daughter!'

All hell broke loose after that, they started brawling. Of course, all the kids were there scared, watching and listening to them smash it out.

My eldest daughter grabbed John's shirt and told him to take his kids.

He called up the next day and said that he was taking the children we had together. Barry told me to say no and to fight for my kids. I prayed and prayed and came to the decision that my two youngest would be better off with him. I was not able to provide for them financially like he could. One thing I am grateful for is that he was able to get them both through a private Catholic primary and high school.

Having my children leave has been one of the hardest things I've ever been through. I would cry for days, and when I visited them I would cry, but tried not to let them see me upset. I needed to be strong and know that I sacrificed my own children to give them a better life.

Many many years passed, my children all grew up. I found it in my heart to forgive. Things ended with Barry, but I am grateful for all that he did for me and especially my children. I am now happier and at peace with my life. Of course, I still regret many things and wonder if I had chosen a different path, would things have been totally different? I cannot change the past, but it has definitely made me a stronger person.

To anyone out there currently going through domestic violence, please know that you are not alone. Please don't be scared. I know it is hard, but you must stay strong. Unfortunately, it took me eight years to get out of that relationship, but there were many lessons learnt. If there are any red flags, please don't avoid them.

Leave as early as you can. There is always a light at the end of a tunnel. Don't be afraid to reach out to friends, family, professional helpers, hotlines. I wish I was more educated, but there is so much more support in this day and age.

Try not to live your life with regrets, because I do. I regret putting my children through all this. They witnessed pretty much every black eye, every court hearing, every bloody nose, every swear word and every heartache.

For me, what got me through was that I learnt to forgive. Forgive myself and forgive all my partners who abused me and that's when I was able to move forward with my life. You are worthy of being happy, and never forget that.

Thank you to my mum who is watching over me. I did everything I could to make my mum happy and proud. I do believe in karma, and I am grateful that my kids are so good to me.

To my beautiful children, Mummy is so proud of each one of you. I am so proud of how you all turned out despite the circumstances we all went through. I'm so sad that I was not able to give you guys more when you needed me the most.

I'm sorry I was not able to support you all financially, but I am very proud that you didn't need to depend on me, and you all have achieved great things. The one thing that I was able to give you, and will always give, is my love. Most of you are parents now and I love all your children. My heart is full knowing that you understand what it is like to love your children wholeheartedly.

I am so sorry I was not strong enough to leave sooner and I'm sorry you all had to witness the abuse for so long. I love you guys so much, and again, Mummy is so proud. *Joop joop.*

Broken

BROKEN.
Tigerlily

My dad would take me fishing out in the boat, far out on the ocean ... and he'd ask me, 'What do you see?'

And I'd say, 'Absolutely nothing! Only the blue sky and sea, blending forever into infinity.'

Dad: 'Now how big do you look in this world?'

Me: 'Super small.'

Dad: 'So how big are your problems in life?'

Me: 'This big,' as I put my thumb and pointer finger together, a millimetre apart.

Dad: 'Well, when you look at the big picture, you realise your problems are not that big and guess what ... right now, you haven't got a worry in the world ... except for catching fish!'

Whenever life's rogue waves try to knock me off my feet, I go down to the ocean, get my bare feet in the sand and draw energy from the earth. I look at the sea and sky and remind myself of Dad's words of wisdom ... my worries are small ... and life's not that tough!

Little did I know, my world would come crashing down as I got slam dunked by a big tsunami wave. I suddenly felt the weight of the whole world, raining down on my shoulders ...

My father is off to court tomorrow for a shitload of paedophile charges. My mum is by his side as the staunch, loving, dutiful wife ... This is her role ... it's what she's always done her whole married life ... I will be by her side, holding her hand. Not to support my old man, but to support her. She's a strong woman, but right now, she needs all the strength and courage I can muster. A shitstorm is brewing and it's about to hit the fan!

I have lost both my parents, some family members, and friends ... but not by death. My old man's been charged with sickening acts on innocent girls. And for the life of them, they cannot get their head around it. Well, we all can't ... we are all in shock and totally shattered.

If I wanted Mum to stay in my life, I had to support him, stand up and shout out his innocence ... even if I had to pretend, just for Mum's sake.

But I couldn't do it. It crossed the boundaries of my beliefs on paedophilia, big time! I was cast out and it felt like I was the one on trial even though I didn't do anything wrong. I lost my mum when I made the decision not to support Dad ... but I still miss her big time ... she was my best friend. I lost my dad, who was my lifetime fishing buddy.

One of the last conversations I had with him, I said, 'You're sick in the head if you have done what they are charging you with. If you have done anything wrong, grow some balls, man up, tell the truth and confess. Don't drag Mum through the courts and have her listen to all the sexual offences you're charged with. She's too old for any more hurt.'

He turned around and replied, 'Well maybe I am sick in the head.' He turned his back on me and started gardening. I knew then in my gut, at that moment, he was guilty.

But he still dragged Mum through the courts, with her as his most staunch and loving supporter. But there was too much evidence, and it got to the point where he had no choice but to plead guilty. Mum blamed the lawyer ... and me.

They say blood is thicker than water, but there are times in life where you must make a choice for your own self-worth. The family not only cut ties with me, but severed them, because I refused to be bullied or emotionally blackmailed into standing up for my old man and defending his innocence.

I have my own beautiful growing tribe now, and they come above and beyond the family I was born into. My role is teaching my kids and grandkids right from wrong ... Stand proud in your truth, beliefs and boundaries.

My mum believes I'm behind the girls coming forward. Her head's been filled with lies and untruths, to try and justify his innocence, and he is the poor picked-on victim. She refuses to talk to me and blames me that he is in jail. It's easier to accept this scenario, rather than acknowledge you've got a sexual predator in the family.

What choice does Mum have? If she accepted the cold hard facts and harsh truth about her husband, it would absolutely destroy and kill her. The only consolation and upside is that I'm keeping her alive and breathing. So, I carry the cape of the scapegoat to protect her from the heartbreaking, hurtful reality. And I understand why family and friends want to blame me, as it's easier to fathom and accept, rather than acknowledge the reality – that he's sick in the head and took advantage of innocent girls. I protect them all from facing the facts by wearing my heavy scapegoat coat.

None of them wanted to hear my side of the story, that I had nothing to do with him being convicted. How could you believe your husband, father, brother, uncle or friend had committed sexual acts and took advantage of innocent girls. He was a lovable character and did so much for the community. I, too, still struggle to believe it in my head. It hurts like hell and it's hard to accept the facts, when you consider someone you love so much had such sickening behaviour traits within him. There is a level of denial in our minds, when we think there is no way he could have committed these heartbreaking, horrifying exploitations. It's so hard to get your head around it. He has the gift of the gab, so can talk his way out of a dodgy or awkward situation. But not this time … the karma train finally caught up with him … as it does in life.

I grudgingly wear the cape of the scapegoat … The heavy weight has nearly broken my spirit, as the life I once knew crumbled down around me. But my love of the earth and ocean (which Dad passed on to me), has been my sanity and saviour. It's where I go to get grounded and let the wind and waves wash away the heaviness on my shoulders … My kids and close friends have kept my head above water, when at times, I felt like drowning in the depths of depression.

Mum couldn't get her head around it, so I understand why she had to blame someone … her loyalty lies in God and her husband. She was raised by the bible … marriage is for life …

'To have and to hold from this day forward, for better for worse, for richer for poorer, in sickness and in health, till death do us part, according to God's holy law. In the presence of God I make this vow … So help me, God! Amen.'

It's pretty fucked up when you think about it. No matter what, you are committed to marriage even when you know in your heart, and your gut instincts are screaming at you, that something isn't right … and RUN! Run away fast, so they can't see you for dust!

It nearly destroyed me, living with the guilt of not bowing down to family expectations and not being there for Mum. In a weird, twisted way, it's now given me strength to stay grounded and stand my truth, no matter what rogue waves come along to try and knock me off my feet. I also draw my strength from Mum, as she is one of the strongest women I know (except when it came to her husband's antics). She taught me to be totally independent, when we only had her in our life, when Dad went 'gallivanting'.

I understand now why she used to say, 'Love all ... marry none. And the big one, 'Men's brains are ruled by their penises.' Pretty bloody harsh, but looking back on her lived experiences, no wonder she thought of men in this way.

How do you deal with a father who's sick in the head? How can you understand a mother who continues to stand by his side, regardless of his sins? It's because she's been trained and conditioned to do so. It's her God-given duty, as a child of God, and his wife ... 'Till death do us part.'

They say no-one gets between a mother and daughter's bond. But what if the devil in sheep's clothing has the power, with his magical, mesmerising charm to break that bond?

How fucked up is it when the devil you're dealing with is your dad. He has the most beautiful heart, but can charm the pants off the unsuspecting when he casts his magic spell. It's fucked up how he groomed my mum to switch off as he pursued his sexual fetishes. A master at throwing around bucketloads of bullshit to cover his tracks. He groomed us all to only see the good ... and he was the 'man of the house'. We wouldn't dare question it, as we were raised in a patriarchal family, one in which the men have most or all the power and importance.

I have seen enough to know that what he's done is derived from a selfish, delusional, sick sense of mind.

I've been shouted down a few times, for standing up when his distorted, disrespectful behaviour towards females, no matter their age, pushed the boundaries. His loving, flamboyant, flirtatious, mesmerising, enchanting, eccentric personality overshadowed his sleazy mouth and sexual innuendos. I got shouted down and told I was overreacting or dramatising when I spoke up ...

'Oh, it's just who he is, he's harmless. All talk and no action,' they'd say. And whenever I questioned his behaviour when he pushed the boundaries, I was told it was my vivid imagination, or I was making up stories. Or I've never forgiven him for having an affair when we were young (another wild story)! Well, look where he is now.

Apparently, my old man's forgiven me. For what? I'm not the one who put him behind bars. But sadly, this is how an emotional manipulator works. They rally the troops and convince everyone of their innocence and put the guilt trip on you, to the point where you'll question your own reality ... and sanity.

'He's only guilty of hugging and giving comfort to the girls ... and in this day and age, that's a criminal offence.' An easier pill to swallow than to face the facts head-on ... so you're blindsided by fairytale fiction.

I still have burning questions ... Has he acknowledged his sins for tampering with innocent girls? Has he apologised and said sorry to them and asked for their forgiveness? Has he said sorry to Mum and the family and told them I'm not to blame? Does he accept that he is the only one accountable for his actions?

Sadly, I will never know the answers as he will probably take it to his grave. My hurdle to jump over, is throwing my scapegoat cape in the air and letting it fly away in the wind. Letting go of giving a fuck, and people's perspective of me, is hard.

There are too many people in society who are under the misconception that domestic abuse is only physical. Tragically, the scars of mental and emotional abuse run deep ... and it bruises the shit out of your heart and soul. Abusers play games, play tricks with your mind and fuck with your sanity. We might not even realise we're being emotionally manipulated, as master manipulators are excellent gaslighters.

They can be conniving con artists, twisting the truth and cleverly convincing others they are totally innocent, and they are the victim. There is no empathy or remorse towards who they hurt unless it can be used to their advantage, or to get out of a sticky situation. I believe, in his head, he still doesn't think he did anything really bad or wrong. My heart aches for the girls he took advantage of … Sadly, some even see he's done no wrong as he 'loved' them … and they 'loved' him. I am genuinely sorry, with all my heart. my father took advantage of these girls.

My heart cries out in pain to all the victims of sexual abuse. They carry their battle scars for life. The ones who stay silent, for fear of not being believed, or being blamed because it must have been their fault, or they must have encouraged it … or craved the attention. I take my hat off to the ones who are brave enough to stand up and fight for their own self-worth in court, even though they may be torn to shreds by the opposing lawyer, family and friends. Every sexual abuse victim has a very heavy burden to carry.

My heart aches for all the women like my mum, who couldn't break the sickening cycle, because they too have been groomed. Lifetimes of conditioning covered with sugar-coated bullshit. Bow down, blinkers on and keep your mouth shut … The patriarchal way. How sad and totally tragic, this still happens in our society today … It sucks balls.

Enough is enough! The buck stops here. I stand my ground and draw a line in the sand. We must all put a big full stop on all forms of domestic abuse. Too many have forgotten … a woman's worth and our vaginas are sacred. Without women, the birth mothers of life, none of us would be breathing. We are goddesses of the world. Love and respect for both sexes should be paramount for all of us and practiced daily, in everyday life … and taught to our kids.

We buried my father the other day ... it was a tough one to attend.

The energy was mixed, with certain family and friends looking at me as if I'm the one to blame for everything that happened. I felt I was on trial for him going to prison ... and his death. But I stood strong and proud as I spoke at his funeral, my kids standing behind me with support and strength. I shared the beautiful, funny and adventurous memories, even though I wanted to scream out my innocence and that they all know deep down that he was the only one accountable for his actions ... and show some fucking remorse and empathy for his victims ... But I held my tongue. As you do at a funeral.

I sat down next to Mum, hugging her and holding her hand throughout the service ... a long time coming. We cried, we laughed, and I felt her soften. I felt her walls of anger and self-protection, ever so slowly coming down ... and then my daughter, cousins and I laughed and danced in front of everyone to his favourite song ... We sent him off the only way we know how ... wild, free-spirited, happy hippy women. Goddesses! He would have loved it ...

> **LIFE HAS TAUGHT ME I AM NOT IN CONTROL. LIFE IS FULL OF EXPERIENCES, LESSONS, HEARTBREAK AND PAIN. BUT IT HAS SHOWN ME LOVE, BEAUTY, POSSIBILITY, AND NEW BEGINNINGS. EMBRACE IT ALL. IT MAKES US WHO WE ARE, AND AFTER EVERY STORM COMES A CLEAR SKY. – UNKNOWN**

and probably would have tried to join us if they hadn't closed the curtains! Lol.

The nightmare and heartache of pain we are carrying is easing slightly, as we pick up the pieces, reconnect to the place of peace in our hearts and slowly begin to heal. I feel the weight of my cape of the scapegoat flying away on the wind as we turn the page and begin a new chapter, creating fresh, funny and beautiful memories …

We all come into this world as innocent human beings and we all have good inside of us. My nanna used to say, 'There is good in everyone … but sometimes you have to dig a bit deeper to find it.' I really had to dig deep to find Dad's good side again. Fuck, it was hard! There is light and dark in all of us, but the trick is to find the balance of Yin and Yang. The badness, the beauty … interconnected and interdependent in the natural world, beautifully balanced … But know your boundaries!

If we ever find we are drawn down into the darkness of evil, we do have the strength in our heart and soul to fight it off. But if you can't slay the devilish antics within yourself … seek professional help – pronto!

I thank both my parents for giving me the breath of life. For raising me on a very colourful journey of love, epic experiences and awesome adventures. The good, the bad, the ugly … and the sad, touches all our lives … It is all intertwined. They are our life lessons and guide us to grow.

I walk proudly forward, taking only the good from my parents, gaining knowledge from the bad, ugly and sad, which I carry with unconditional love inside of me. It's what makes me the woman I am today … I may be scarred, but I'm not broken. I wear my battle scars proudly, as I radiate a sensitive and beautiful inner strength, that shines bright from the depths of my heart and soul.

There is always daylight after darkness … I pass my life's

experiences, adventurous stories and growing wisdom onto my kids, grandkids, and anyone else who cares to listen ...

Love, light and wisdom,
Tigerlily

NOTES

- The role of the scapegoat is usually assigned to the most sensitive, outspoken, different child (that's me ... I'm all of these).
- Evil is the use of power to destroy the spiritual growth of others for the purpose of defending and preserving the integrity of our own sick selves. In short, it is scapegoating. – M Scott Peck
- Scapegoating – the act of blaming a person for something bad that someone else has done. – *Cambridge Dictionary*

Survivor

SURVIVOR.
Jennifer

It's all a distant memory and to this day I wonder why we recall certain events more than others, but they're there quietly lying dormant till the dark curtains are drawn back. Stored in the depths of my soul, where it reveals a timid, frail little voice crying out helplessly for someone to stop the force, the thudding in my ears, with each pound that unleashed on to her delicate frame. My mother limp and lifeless on the stair floor. What little could I do, I did with all my might, my tiny hands gripping onto his lower leg, begging my father to stop. I begged for my life, for my mother's life, 'Bo moun di tu Khong?' Do you want to go to prison? Then please stop! The tears streamed down my face; I had never felt more alone.

It never does stop, they never will stop, it never stops there, it's been thirty years since it happened, I'm now thirty-seven and the trauma of that frightful day lingers on serving its purpose. It's extended this far with my biological father still in prison, my mother served four and a half years. I can only hope this heavy veil of suffering lifts, hopefully it's not forever, hopefully not till I take my last breath, this last breath called life.

Those scarring seconds carry on into every moment of my life, every step and second, it's every shortness of breath, until it's all I know. It's tiring and debilitating, suffocating, just as I thought life is as good as it gets, it grabs me by the throat, making me revisit my hell on earth, in those dark places banging on my door asking God why did you put me here in the first place even if it's not your fault.

I had no choice to live under the conditions life had set out for me. After we fled Sydney to start a new life in Perth my parents were incarcerated. At fifteen, I started my life in Perth without the guidance and love of my mother and stepfather – well as loving as heroin drug-trafficking parents could be. They were put away, so here was my chance to live my life normally, as normal as I imagined and dreamed it could and would be.

What was even normal anymore, sixteen and I've borne the scars, quietly dreaming of one day being set free from the chains of child rape and molestation, abandonment, drugs, violence, abuse, broken friendships, schools and friends that I would never see again. Where was I to start over from the pits of my despair. I was completely broken.

What was worse, my boyfriends would have never understood any of it, and what would they know at sixteen? I was in my second relationship, with my first love left back in a Sydney Prison.

Little did I know, I would have etched my trauma onto my boyfriends, leading them

> **"MY ORDEAL HAS BEEN A JOURNEY, IT'S OPENED UP WOUNDS I DON'T KNOW IF I CAN EVER HEAL FROM. TRAUMATIC IN WAYS THE MIND COULD NOT FATHOM, STRESSFUL TO NEAR DEATH AND SEEMINGLY IMPOSSIBLE TO OVERCOME.**

into volatile nights of arguments, isolation, not seeing friends or family. Events where people coexisted and got together anything remotely social was a no-go zone. It didn't last, it reached breaking point, I wanted to leave. 'Leave?' he said, in a rush of emotions, tension filled the air, things were thrown, push came to shove, I fell to the floor, my knee split open. Blood filled the floor, the cut left me wide and vulnerable, bleeding from a violent wound reflecting all the pain I've gone through, left for all to see.

I was absolutely miserable and it was a recipe for disaster, relationship after relationship, it got worse and worse. The cycle of violence follows me everywhere I go. Is it me, is it my fault, I don't deserve this, how do I find myself faced with abuse, this must be all I know, all I attract, will it ever end?

The darkness chased me like a plague terrorising me in my sleep. I couldn't sleep night after night. I recall the ringing on my cheek, the swelling from the righteous hand impacting my face, torching the surface to oblivion. With each violent episode my mind took me on flight mode. I had to leave, I had to pack my things and end it at all costs, this time it cost me my first baby – sixteen and pregnant with my abuser. I lost my baby – the tears rolled down and I felt the world throw me out on the curb. It was only eighteen years later that I mourned her death, the pain and loss consumed my soul, there was no release from the suffering. I found solace in sketching her face, and telling her I love her and her sister so much, that this life wasn't meant for her, that I'm sorry, sorry forever.

As a survivor, time heals all things, believing in making a difference can only work with you, it's never too late to start over. Self-love can get us through, embrace it, allow it to show up, it's powerful in ways you never knew, let it work for you. You have a choice to make the right decision, even when it's a bad choice, just make one, stick to it and never regret your choice. Having no choice is still a choice. Believing in yourself, anyway, no-one believes in you more than you. Where you are in life is no coincidence, it's all been a choice, the more you see that, the more powerful your choices become, the more clearly you own who you are and the potential you have to create all you want.

Lastly and most importantly, 'love yourself'.

Money makes the world go round, as does many things. Take note, be aware of what does, break the cycle, if you can see it, feel it, touch it, then you can let it go. Don't hold onto toxic fuel.

ZONTA HOUSE.
Kelda

Every day is different. Every minute is different. You can be fist-pumping, celebrating a win one moment and wanting to cry and scream at the injustice in another. I was naive – I thought I knew what family and domestic violence was, what it felt like, and what I wanted to do to make the world a better place. I never knew that a job, that an organisation, that a social issue or that survivors would change my life so considerably. I have been working in a leadership position at a women's refuge organisation for over eight years, but all my life I have been surrounded by courageous, intelligent women and survivors. Women who have resisted the violence and abuse every step of the way. Survivors of terror and abuse at the hands of perpetrators that should have loved, cherished and cared for them.

Family and domestic violence is a deliberate action: perpetrators choose to abuse and perpetrate violence upon victims and survivors, and strategically work to repress their acts of resistance. Family and domestic violence is prevalent in our community. Every day we see the terror, abuse and harm being inflicted in our neighbourhoods. The effect is devastating – emotionally, physically, mentally and financially. We know, we understand and see the isolation, devastation and trauma this societal issue causes. But what we also see is the damage and trauma done by institutions and services in response to survivors and perpetrators.

There are days and moments that are overwhelming where I think – *Why and how can we do this? Are we making a difference – AM I making a difference?* But I get up and keep going – one foot after the other. Why? Because women and children deserve to feel safe in their homes and live free from abuse and violence. And until then, I want to make sure that if they do need help, support or for someone to hold the hope for a moment, that they have a service or response of quality. That the service or response is there for them and whatever they need. I also want to contribute to shifting those entrenched attitudes and systems that enable the abuse and violence to thrive. We need to put the onus back on to those perpetrating and supporting this behaviour – not constantly blaming or shifting back to the responsibility of victims and survivors. I want to live in a community that is actively resisting and working towards stopping family and domestic violence, holding perpetrators accountable and providing space for safety and recovery for victims and survivors.

It is an interesting place to balance something you feel so passionate and dedicated about and it being a job, especially when we have staff that are working every second of every day. As an organisation we must have strong governance and financial control, safety policies and practices, and we need to be sustainable, but driven by our purpose. We have comprehensive systems in place, and we are constantly improving, adjusting and responding to the community. All decisions made now and into our future come down to fitting in and achieving our purpose. We need to remember why we are here and who we are here to serve and support.

We operate refuges for women offering a suite of support, education and advocacy programs, with the whole focus on supporting women to navigate the many systems to leave their situation, or after leaving, and most of all to support recovery. Family and domestic violence does not discriminate, and this is evident in the diversity of women who access our services. Women from all walks of life, women of all ages and women from across the world. We want all of our services to feel like and be safe places for women to be themselves, a place free of judgement, a place of trust and a place where they can start to heal. The women are always the experts in their own journeys – we just sometimes help to let their voices be heard.

There is often talk about the impact of family and domestic violence, and what I have come to learn is; whatever your response is or how you cope, is normal. There is no right or wrong way to survive. Sometimes just having a safe place to sleep, to know you don't need to walk on eggshells is all someone needs – just respite. Other times women are supported over longer periods of time. Our services recognise this, and we have different programs women can access across time. We know the statistics and research, we understand why it isn't always as easy as just leaving. We know that sometimes it is just too unsafe to leave, they aren't ready or our services aren't suitable at this moment in time. What I do hope is that in their time with us – whether it be one night, one appointment, a conversation or one workshop – we have provided that someone with a plan, with information or with an affirmation that they can reach out again whenever or wherever they are. We are fortunate to see women reclaim their independence, thrive and take strides in recovery and healing. Seeing women engaged in the community, in their own homes, feeling safe and working towards their own goals is so powerful. It is a privilege and honour to walk alongside every woman.

What is inspiring is seeing the power, confidence and support women get from each other. Women being together in solidarity, whether it be small moments of cooking, eating, dancing, singing, yarning, celebrating wins or just simply sitting in silence together. Over and over again women say one of the greatest learnings they took from our programs was being with other women who have had similar experiences, with no judgement.

There is hope. There is a shift. We are seeing more and more goodwill in the community. People, groups and organisations reaching out to see how they can help. Government announcements and commitments to increase funding. Corporate organisations implementing policies and training. An increased focus on perpetrator accountability and change in legislation across the country. Is it enough? Not yet. We need to see comprehensive investment across the spectrum, and we need to address the underlying drivers and causes of family and domestic violence and challenge the behaviours and attitudes that underpin and enable family and domestic violence. But, in the meantime, we continue to listen, support, advocate and stand alongside others to provide safety and healing. And maybe together, one step at a time, we can walk towards a better and safer world for us all.

KO
www.zontahouse.org.au

METTLE WOMEN INC.

Bronwyn

Mettle, by definition, is to face adversity with spirit and resilience. It's something that I have the privilege of witnessing every day. I work alongside women who have fled their homes as a result of domestic and family violence. Women who would be completely forgiven for throwing up their hands and saying, 'I give up.' Somehow, these brave women still show up every day and fill our workplace with joy and optimism.

Mettle Gifts is a registered charity that operates a national gift delivery service. We are staffed by women who are referred to us by our partner crisis refuges when they're ready to start rebuilding the safe, financially secure life that they deserve. Through paid work placements and training, we support these women to unlock their true potential, attain financial independence, and find and secure their own safe housing. We also provide participants with access to wraparound support such as food insecurity services, subsidised child care support, psychological support, interpreters (for CALD women), transport subsidies and study scholarships.

After years of working in the non-profit space I was so saddened to see that despite the stellar efforts of frontline service providers, 52% of women and children residing in crisis accommodation as a result of domestic and family violence had been there before. Mettle is the product of a year of research with survivors around

Australia to find out why they were returning to homelessness and abuse. With these courageous women, the Mettle business plan was designed to act as a mechanism to get women facing homelessness back into the workforce when it was safe enough to do so and help them to remove the barriers that were making this possible.

Although I have so many beautiful stories to share about the graduates of our program, I think it's most important to share one that highlights the dangerous reality that the women in our care face every day. For the safety of this woman, I've changed her name to Sarah. Sarah was our first ever program participant. She came to work for us after residing in a crisis refuge with her sixteen-year-old son for nine months. She has endured thirty-three years of horrendous abuse and suffered tragically from the shortfalls of the justice system. After six months of working with us, and navigating some incredibly traumatic court cases, she saved enough for a bond and moved into her own safe apartment. We put Sarah through TAFE so that she could complete her year ten studies, something she was never allowed to do before. Sarah unlocked a love for learning and went on to complete her studies in community services. One year on and Sarah is completing her Diploma of Counselling. On a mission to help women who are facing what she once endured. Although Sarah takes large strides forward, her perpetrator continues to breach his Violence Restraining Order and put Sarah's life at risk every day. The system needs to be reformed to protect brilliant women like Sarah and her family.

I had the honour of meeting Sheree when I was conducting the preliminary research for the Mettle business model. I wanted to ensure that our structure was informed by the lived experience of a range of women around Australia. Sheree generously agreed to share how domestic and family violence had impacted her life and what systematic failures needed to change. Sheree's warmth and openness was unparalleled and I asked if she would help us launch as a survivor ambassador. The support and advocacy that Sheree and Yasmin has provided our young organisation is more than we could ever have asked for and we are eternally grateful for the voice that they give to women not just here in WA, but around the nation. To be involved in this book is a privilege we are thankful for.

Bronwyn Bate, CEO and founder – Mettle Women INC.
www.mettlegifts.com

CONCLUSION.
Emma Weaver

Domestic abuse can happen to anyone. There is no strict profile for victims, however, there can be for perpetrators. Abuse can be subtle at the start and can take you by surprise – always an excuse, a justification for their actions, they are the victim – didn't you know? Alienation, comments on your dress, your weight, words like *you did not use to be like this* can start to play on your mind and slowly chip at your confidence, eventually leading you to the point of confusion and loneliness within you, where you do not even know reality from lies and patterns of behaviour. Self-doubt and lack of self-worth become familiar thoughts in your head. Do not ask, do not question and certainly do not have an opinion.

If you were not fortunate enough in childhood to know what a healthy relationship is, you can perhaps understand why, in adulthood, we may fall prey to the same abusive relationships and patterns of behaviours – therefore repeating the cycle of generations before. The hidden world behind closed doors is not spoken about often enough, and the brave women in this book share their powerful stories of abuse, guilt, shame, confusion, but above all else, courage – courage beyond their wildest dreams to come away from toxic situations and relationships, and are still here telling their stories providing hope and comfort to others.

CONCLUSION.

Working in mental health for over twenty-two years, I have witnessed firsthand the impact enduring domestic violence can have on victims – these can be partners, children and parents. Over 46.2% of people spend between two and ten years with an abusive partner, and over 17% stay longer than ten. *(Source: womensaid.org.uk)*

Depression, anxiety, PTSD, heightened fear, social withdrawal and substance misuse can all be effects of domestic violence and can be felt for years after the relationship has ended. Support is vital to healing and recovery. Counselling plays a huge part when overcoming the impact of abuse, whether it was in childhood witnessing abuse, being abused as a child or as an adult. The psychological impact can be lasting. There are many different therapies available, and working in mental health services, and while I was on the BOD for Fermanagh Women's Aid, I witnessed firsthand the positive impact these can have on those who have survived abuse. We want to not only survive abuse, we want to thrive and create a meaningful life afterwards.

Speaking to your GP, a friend or a health visitor can often be the first step to freeing yourself from the situation – I cannot express enough how important that first step is. Find someone that you can tell and try not to think too much forward, just know that you are doing the right thing reaching out.

Rapid transformational therapy (RTT) is often available for support in the healing journey and when a person is willing to face the issues that have come with the impact of abuse.

Counselling and psychotherapy is another support that is extremely important when dealing with the after-effects of abuse. Working on the issues, and releasing those feelings that are often associated with all types of abuse, allows survivors to begin a new journey in their lives. Women's aid, support groups, and mother and baby groups are all supportive environments that are important as we need to feel supported and heard. Quite often abuse goes unnoticed and people's voices are not heard or even believed. Your feelings are valid, you did not deserve the abuse and you did the best that you could at the time. Supportive environments where people may have experienced the same can be powerful in your journey and road to freedom. Much like the brave women in this book.

Learning the difference between a healthy and an unhealthy relationship is paramount in life from a young age, and especially after experiencing abuse. Speaking from lived experience, as the people in this book are, and education in school is vital to reduce domestic violence. Know the signs.

Signs of a healthy relationship:
- *Mutual respect.* Respect means that each person values the other and understands the other person's boundaries.
- *Trust.* Partners should place trust in each other and give each other the benefit of the doubt.
- *Honesty.* Honesty builds trust and strengthens the relationship.
- *Compromise.* In a dating relationship, each partner does not always get their way. Each should acknowledge different points of view and be willing to give and take.
- *Individuality.* Neither partner should have to compromise who they are, and their identity should not be based on a partner's. Each should continue seeing their own friends and doing the things they love.
- *Good communication.* Each partner should speak honestly and openly to avoid miscommunication. If one person needs to sort out their feelings first, the other partner should respect those wishes and wait until they are ready to talk.

- *Arguing fair.* Everyone argues at some point, but those who are fair, stick to the subject and avoid insults are more likely to come up with a possible solution.
- *Understanding.* Each partner should take time to understand what the other might be feeling.
- *Healthy sexual relationship.* Dating partners engage in a sexual relationship that both are comfortable with, and neither partner feels pressured or forced to engage in sexual activity that is outside their comfort zone or without consent.

These are some examples of a healthy relationship – one where you feel loved, valued, respected, heard and where you are not afraid.

An unhealthy relationship can look very different and some signs to look out for can be:
- *Jealousy and Possessiveness.* Wants to be with you constantly. Accuses you of cheating all the time. Follows you around and frequently calls. Asks friends to check up on you.
- *Controlling Behaviour.* Constantly questions who you spend your time with, what you did/wore/said, where you went. Makes you ask permission to do certain things. Acts like you don't have the ability to make good decisions. Hides controlling behaviour by pretending to be concerned for your safety.
- *Quick Involvement.* Six months or less before living together or engaged. Claims love at first sight. Pressure for commitment. Says you are the only one who can make them feel this way.
- *Unrealistic Expectations.* Compliments you in a way that makes you seem superhuman. Over-flattering. Expects you to be perfect. Says, 'I am all you need. You are all I need.'
- *Isolation.* Puts down everyone you know – friends are either stupid, slutty, or you are cheating with them – family is too controlling,

- *Blames others for problems.* If there are problems at school or work, it is always someone else's fault. If anything goes wrong in the relationship, it is all your fault. Won't take responsibility for their own behaviour.
- *Hypersensitivity.* Easily insulted. Sees everything as a personal attack. Looks for fights. Blows things out of proportion.
- *Unpredictable.* You can never tell what will upset them.
- *Verbal abuse of any kind.*
- *Rigid sex roles.* Believes women are inferior to men. Unable to be a whole person without a relationship.
- *Dr Jekyll and Mr Hyde.* Sudden mood changes – like they have two personalities. One minute nice, next minute exploding. One minute happy, next minute sad.
- *Past relationships.* You may hear the person was abusive to someone else. They say it's a lie, or their ex was 'crazy', or it wasn't that bad.
- *Threats of any kind.*
- *Breaking or striking objects.* Breaks loved possessions. Beats on table with fists. Throws objects.
- *Any force during an argument.* Pushes, shoves, or physically restrains you from leaving the room.
- *Doesn't respect your property or privacy.*

These are some warning signs that the relationship may not be healthy and you need to be aware of these and consider your relationship. They are not always easy to recognise and once you become aware of them you may already have become used to them and adjusted your lifestyle to accommodate the relationship. Just know if it does not feel right, it isn't. Try to reach out if you can, even so you are not isolated.

One thing all the women in this book speak about are their

feelings throughout. If you are used to not being heard or that your feelings are not valid, you begin to believe that you are not worthy of better. But you are.

There are many different types of abuse, including:
- Psychological
- Physical
- Financial
- Sexual
- Coercive control

Domestic abuse is a pattern of behaviour designed to control another person.

It is important to recognise the pain each woman in this book has come through. The isolation felt and the impact domestic abuse has had on their lives. Each woman with similar experiences, yet so different. Each incident as impactful as the next, and the doubt each person had in their ability to break free from the abuse, the thoughts in their mind that they may be at fault or not believed. Each person let down – perhaps as a child witnessing and enduring abuse, as an adult by friends, neighbours, family or those who witnessed the abuse. Making their strength in the healing journey even more powerful.

It is so important to identify those around you who you can trust – never let anyone take this away. It is equally important when you witness wrong, or someone confides in you, do not turn away in fear, find the same courage and strength these women have and be part of the solution. Help those who need support, listen and believe when someone reaches out.

REFLECTION.

LOVE BRUISES & BULLSHiT.

SUPPORT.

If you are in a life threatening emergency, please call 000 immediately.

1800 RESPECT (1800 737 732)
The National Family & Domestic Violence Line for any Australian who has experienced, or is at risk of, Family & Domestic violence.
24 hours, 7 days a week

LIFELINE (13 11 14)
A national number that can help put you in contact with a crisis service in your state.
24 hours, 7 days a week

RELATIONSHIPS AUSTRALIA (1300 364 277)
Support groups and counselling on relationships, and for abusive and abused partners.

KIDS HELPLINE (1800 55 1800)
Counselling for children and young people.
24 hours, 7 days a week

NATIONAL DISABILITY ABUSE AND NEGLECT HOTLINE (1800 880 052 / TIS:13 14 50 / NRS:1800 55 677)

A national number for reporting abuse and neglect of people with a disability.
9am-9pm weekdays and 10am-4pm weekends

DOMESTIC AND FAMILY VIOLENCE

www.iamsheree.com.au
www.centreforwomen.org.au
www.zontahouse.org.au
www.womenscouncil.com.au
www.patgilescentre.org.au
www.victimsofcrime.wa.gov.au
www.dcp.wa.gov.au
www.dvconnect.org
www.whfs.org.au
www.preventviolence.org.au
www.dvassist.org.au

RELATIONSHIPS/FAMILY

www.familyrelationships.gov.au
www.lifeline.org.au
www.1800respect.org.au
www.raisingchildren.net.au
www.servicesaustralia.gov.au
www.safehelpline.org
www.centrecare.com.au
www.anglicarewa.org.au
www.kidshelpline.com.au
www.communicare.org.au

GENERAL HELPLINES

www.blackdoginstitute.org.au
www.beyondblue.org.au
www.mindspot.org.au
www.suicidecallbackservice.org.au
www.relationships.org.au
www.headspace.org.au
www.sane.org
www.talkspace.com
www.legalaid.wa.gov.au
www.adf.org.au

www.ingramcontent.com/pod-product-compliance
Lightning Source LLC
Chambersburg PA
CBHW022042290426

44109CB00014B/957